weave

weave

Designs by
Wendy Cartwright, Helen Frostell,
Mary Hawkins and Lynne Peebles

MURDOCH BOOKS

contents

techniques

projects

Introduction

Weaving is one of humankind's fundamental skills. Since the earliest times, it has been held in high regard as a professional and honoured craft. By the 11th century, many of the weaving patterns in use today had been invented, and the guild workshops of the Middle Ages were the foundation for textile production in the Industrial Revolution. The advent of new technology resulted in the craft of handweaving ceasing to be a major source of livelihood. However, handwoven articles were still greatly valued.

The craft of weaving, with its many allied crafts, helped shape much of present-day Britain and its history. While the traditions of the craft all but died out during the Industrial Revolution, sufficient remained in rural areas, and in the records of master weavers, to enable a very complete picture to be drawn. The tradition of the weaver as a fine craftsperson, and an inventive one, is still alive and should be maintained.

In some places, handweaving is still a significant, living craft. Using fairly simple tools, very fine cloths — superior to any woven by machine — are produced. In India, silk or cotton cloths worked with real gold thread are woven for saris, while in Scandinavia, the production by hand of woven rugs, curtains and cushions remains a viable commercial proposition.

The early 1970s saw a great resurgence of interest in handweaving and textile arts. Numerous courses became available in universities, technical colleges and community centres. Up until 1970, most handweavers used only two- or four-shaft looms, but with the proliferation of technical courses and weaving classes, eight-shaft looms became popular. Numerous books and magazines on weaving and the fine arts were published and it was very much a boom time for handweavers.

With advanced technology, it is now possible to buy dobby looms and computerized looms. These looms can have as many as 32 shafts and so weaving is becoming more advanced and complicated.

Today's weaver is very fortunate in having access to an ever-expanding range of yarns in both traditional and new fibres, such as soy silk, Tencel, stainless steel and mixtures of wool, silk and stainless steel. A beautifully designed handwoven fabric for clothing or a one-of-a-kind article for the home will always be regarded as special and distinctly different from its mass-produced counterpart. The end product is not the only reward for the craftsperson — creating and making it are just as satisfying.

This sample was woven on a four-shaft loom using a technique developed by Theo Moorman (see page 52), which allows a second weft (here, a mohair loop yarn) to be inlaid over the ground fabric.

Weaving basics

Any piece of woven cloth consists of vertical or longthwise threads, which are known as the warp, interlaced at right angles with horizontal or crosswise threads, called the weft. The first stage of weaving is to measure and wind the warp threads (see pages 12–13). The warp threads are then attached to the loom (see pages 14–15) and put under tension. The weft yarn (which may or may not be the same as the warp yarn) is wound onto a shuttle that is then passed back and forth across the warp to form the cloth.

Every loom has a 'shedding' device; this separates some of the warp threads from the others so that the shuttle carrying the weft thread can be passed through that space, which is known as a shed. Changing between one shed and the other on successive passes serves to interlace the warp and the weft to form the woven fabric. After each pass of the shuttle, the weft thread is packed firmly into place by means of a moving device known as a beater.

A single thread of warp is known as an end. Every weave has a certain number of ends per inch (epi) or ends per centimetre (e/cm); this is the number of ends per inch or per centimetre across the warp. This is also known as the sett; for example, a sett of 20 epi means that there are 20 warp ends per inch. A single thread of weft is known as a pick. Picks per inch (ppi) or picks per centimetre (p/cm) refers to the number of weft threads, or picks, per inch or per centimetre.

The loom has a series of shafts; these horizontal frames serve as the loom's shedding devices. A loom must have at least two shafts to create a shed through which the shuttle can pass. To the shaft are attached heddles — lengths of string or thin metal with a small hole, or 'eye', at the centre, through which a warp end is threaded. In a floor loom, the shafts are attached to treadles, which are operated with the feet. Depending on the sequence in which the treadles are operated, different warp threads are picked up on successive passes of the shuttle; it is these different sequences that produce the pattern of the weave (see also pages 26–27).

Once the entire length of cloth has been woven, it may be hem stitched (see page 28), then it is cut from the loom. Handwoven cloth should be washed and pressed; it can then be used as is (as a scarf, shawl or table runner, for example), or cut up and then sewn into homewares or garments.

There are many different types of loom, and more than one way to prepare a loom. For best results, familiarize yourself thoroughly with your particular loom and its use. The beginner weaver would be well advised to attend a course in weaving; seeing the craft demonstrated will make the process much clearer.

table loom A table loom (the one pictured has eight shafts) is ideal for weavers who lack the space for a floor loom, or who wish to weave only smaller pieces. With a table loom, the shafts are lifted with levers.

floor loom To weave larger pieces or more complex patterns, a floor loom is required. This example has eight shafts; in floor looms, the shafts are lifted and lowered by depressing the treadles.

Looms

Looms vary greatly in size and complexity. Most beginner weavers learn on a table loom and progress to a floor loom. All but three of the projects in this book were created on floor looms, of which there are a number of different types.

Counterbalance Usually limited to four shafts, this loom works with two shafts up and two shafts down. The tie-up is fairly simple but it is difficult to weave unbalanced weaves (see page 16) on this loom.

Countermarch This loom is the most preferred by professional weavers because it will give a perfect shed with any number of shafts. Each shaft works as an independent unit, with the rising and falling controlled by the treadles. The countermarch loom can have from four to 16 shafts.

Jack The simplest of the floor looms, this has four or eight shafts. The shafts rise only (rather than both rising and falling) and so tying them to the treadles is comparatively simple.

Other types of loom

Table looms The most commonly used table looms have four or eight shafts, although table looms with more shafts and with only two shafts are also available.

Small hand looms These looms consist of square or rectangular wooden frames with small nails set in them; yarn is wound around the nails from one side of the loom to the other, in three alternating layers. The final layer, which serves to interlace the fabric, is created using yarn threaded into a long needle. See also pages 30–31.

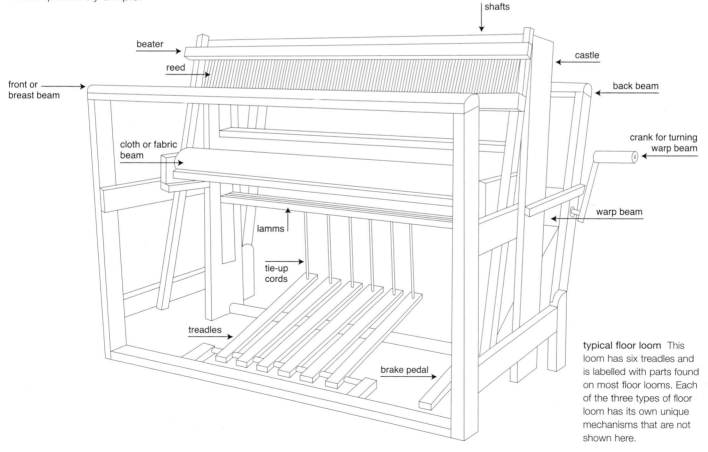

shafts

beater

reed

castle

front or breast beam

back beam

cloth or fabric beam

crank for turning warp beam

lamms

warp beam

tie-up cords

treadles

brake pedal

typical floor loom This loom has six treadles and is labelled with parts found on most floor looms. Each of the three types of floor loom has its own unique mechanisms that are not shown here.

Other equipment

As well as a loom, the following equipment is needed before weaving commences:

Bobbin winder A bobbin winder is designed to wind yarns onto bobbins for use in a boat shuttle. Bobbin winders come in different shapes and with different drive mechanisms, both manual and electric.

Cross sticks When measuring the warp, the cross is the figure-of-eight that is made at both ends of the warp to prevent tangles later on. The cross sticks are used to put in the cross on the warp once it has been removed from the warping board. Threading the warp through the heddles is done from the cross sticks once the warp has been attached to the loom.

Raddle Looms can be warped up from front to back, or back to front. If warping back to front, a raddle is needed. This length of wood has pegs or nails at even intervals, and is used when rolling onto the warp beam to separate and spread the warp to the correct width.

Reed The reed sits inside the beater (see also page 19), and consists of vertical teeth set at regular intervals within a frame. (The teeth used to be made of actual reed, hence their name; now they are either carbon or stainless steel.) Each space in the reed is known as a dent. The reed acts as a spacer for the warp yarn, which is threaded through it, usually one or more threads per dent. Reeds come in various sizes based on the number of dents per inch; most weavers will have

Shuttles

The various types of shuttles are designed for different tasks and uses. Three of the most commonly used are as follows:

Boat shuttle This is the quickest to 'throw' (or to pass through the shed), as the yarn is wound on a bobbin and feeds from it automatically as the shuttle passes through the shed. One disadvantage of boat shuttles is that they cannot hold as much heavy yarn as, for example, a ski shuttle.

Ski shuttle This is used for heavier yarns and rug weaving. The yarn is wound directly onto the shuttle, between two 'horns' on its upper surface, without the use of a bobbin.

Stick shuttle A simple shuttle with a notch in each end through which the yarn is wound; good for carrying small amounts of yarn. These are the cheapest shuttles to buy (and are also easy to make yourself) and come in many styles and lengths. They can be used in narrow or wide warps, and should be a little wider than the weaving. Stick shuttles are also less expensive than other shuttles, as they do not require a bobbin winder.

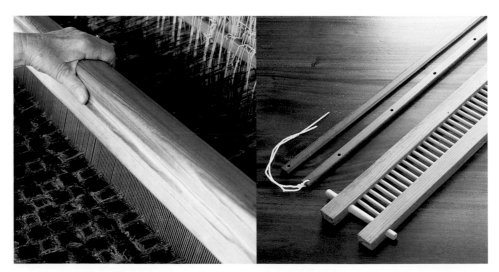

beating The beater, which contains the reed, is used to pack the weft threads into place.

left to right Cross sticks (also known as lease sticks) and a raddle.

several reeds to allow for different setts. Reeds also come in different widths; for example, a 24-inch (60 cm) reed is 24 inches wide and can weave a 24-inch wide warp. A warp is centred on the reed. The term 'sley' means to insert a warp thread through a dent in the reed.

Reed hook This small, flat tool (also known as a sley hook) assists in 'sleying the reed', or pulling the warp through the dents in the reed.

Temple Also known as a stretcher, this tool can be adjusted to various widths and is used to keep the width of a weaving constant.

Threading hook Also known as a warp hook or heddle hook, and used to thread a warp end through a heddle (although some weavers prefer to thread the heddles using their fingers).

Warping board Before the warp is attached to the loom, it must first be measured. This is the purpose of a warping board, a square or rectangular frame with a series of pegs around the outside. A warping mill (see page 12) performs a similar function to a warping board but is generally used for longer warps. Either tool permits a long warp to be measured in a very compact way. The required length of warp is calculated, and then the warp thread is passed back and forth between a series of pegs to give the correct length for one end of warp. This process is continued until enough thread has been wound for the required number of warp ends; the warp is then transferred to the loom (see page 14). See pages 12–13 for more detailed instructions on using a warping board.

small looms For very compact and portable weaving, small looms are ideal. The one pictured produces squares measuring 4 in (10 cm). Such looms can be found under various proprietary names, including Weave-It. Small looms of other dimensions, as well as rectangular and triangular versions, are also available. See pages 30–33 for instructions on weaving with a small loom, and pages 82 and 102 for projects using small-loom squares.

left to right Boat shuttle, bobbin winder, stick shuttle, threading hook, stick shuttle, ski shuttle.

warping mill Here, the cross can be seen around the two pegs at the top and bottom.

Using a warping board

Warping boards have a number of pegs and holes so the pegs can be moved around depending on the length of the warp. The pegs are about 5 in (13 cm) apart. The distance between a peg on the left side of the warping board and one on the right side is usually a standard measure (for example, one yard or one metre, or half that), making it easy to work out how many pegs must be traversed to give the correct warp length. If constructing your own warping board, keep this in mind when designing it.

If threading the loom with a raddle, the cross is usually made around the first two and last two pegs on the warping board. If threading from front to back, it is easier to have a distance between the cross and the end of the warp — say 5 in (13 cm).

Warping

The simplest way to wind a warp is on a warping board. Most warping boards will take up to about 10 metres or 10 yards of warp. However, when winding a longer warp, a warping mill is used. The most important thing when winding a warp is the cross (also known as the lease); this is the intersection between one warp end and the next, and is made by taking the yarn in a figure-of-eight pattern around the last two pegs on the warping board, so that the yarn crosses over itself. The purpose of the cross is to keep the ends separate and secure, and to prevent tangles later. The warp is best wound with a cross each end for safety, so that if one cross comes undone you still have another.

Setting up the guide string

Before winding the warp, you will need to work out the path that your warp will take on the board. First, calculate the required length of one warp end. If using one of the projects in this book, the required warp length is given in the instructions; if making up your own project, see page 22 for how to calculate warp length. Cut a piece of waste yarn this length, plus enough extra to allow for tying both ends to the pegs. This will be your guide string; make it a contrasting colour from the warp yarn so that it is easily distinguished.

warping board Yarn is wound around the pegs to a pre-determined length to create the warp.

guide string Here, the guide string (in red) can be seen under the wound warp.

counting thread Showing a counting thread inserted in the warp.

Tie one end of the guide string to one of the pegs on the warping board. Next, find a path on the warping board that produces the correct warp length. Once you have found a correct path, tie the other end of the guide string in place. You are now ready to wind the warp, following the path of the guide string.

When winding the warp, put in a counting thread every 1 in (2.5 cm) or, say, every 10 or 20 warp ends. This helps to count the number of warp ends and makes it easy to spread the warp evenly in the raddle to the correct width. If the first pass is made from top to bottom of the warping board, the second pass is made from bottom to top. Continue in this manner until you have wound the correct number of warp ends. If you need to join in a new cop or cone of yarn, always make the join at either end of the warp, using a knot. Avoid any knots in the middle of the warp. Before removing the warp from the board, tie the cross securely (see right) to maintain the order in which the warp has been wound.

Tying the cross

Before removing the warp from the warping board, it is vital to tie the cross securely so that it does not come undone while the warp is being transferred to the loom or during tying on. Ties should be made on either side of the cross, as shown in the photograph below, and also around the cross itself.

Chaining the warp

When removing the warp from the warping board or mill, it is formed into a chain, which keeps it from becoming tangled, especially if it will not be used immediately. To chain the warp, make a loop in one end, then draw the body of the warp threads through the loop to form another loop (as though making crochet chains). Continue in this manner along the length of the warp. To stop the chain from unravelling, make a tie between the last loop and the unchained end of the warp.

cross ties Showing a tie on either side of the cross to help keep it secure.

chaining the warp Make a loop in the bundle of threads, then draw the threads through the loop.

the chained warp Continue in this manner along the length of the warp.

threading Showing warp ends threaded through the heddles.

Threading up and tying on

The process of putting the warp on the loom is known as 'dressing' the loom. The warp is threaded from the cross, with each thread being taken in the same order in which the warp was wound. This stops the threads from becoming tangled with each other.

The loom can be dressed from back to front or front to back; each weaver will choose the method that best suits him or herself, and the particular loom. Whatever method is used, the warp should always be centred in the loom, so it is necessary to know the width of the warp in the reed. Always check before threading up that the reed is centred in the beater. It is a good idea to mark the centre of the reed, either by tying a thread in the centre of the reed, or by marking the centre of the beater with a marking pen. Also mark the centre of the beater frame — this mark will ensure that you hold the beater in the centre to beat.

Dressing the loom from back to front

This method requires a raddle, which is essentially a coarse reed with round pegs, and is used to distribute the warp evenly across the warp beam. Some raddles have a removable cap, which is used to keep all the threads in place.

tying on Pass two groups of ends under the stick, which is tied to the apron.

tying on, continued Bring the groups up and around the stick, then tie them together.

tying on completed Proceed along the width of the beam until all ends are tied on.

You will also need cardboard or paper, or preferably warp sticks, inserted between the layers of warp. This is to prevent the warp yarn from biting down unevenly through the layers of threads and to prevent threads at the edge of the warp from slipping off. Cross sticks (see also pages 10 and 19) are inserted in the cross and are used to help thread the warp ends in the correct order through the heddles.

To begin dressing the loom, push the heddles on all the shafts well away to both sides, and work from the back of the loom. Remove the stick that is tied to the apron on the back beam and thread the loops at the end of the warp evenly onto the stick. Then reattach the stick to the apron.

Centre the raddle and attach it to the loom, then spread the warp evenly across the raddle using the counting thread (see page 13). Attach the cap of the raddle (if it has one) to keep the threads in place.

Once these steps are completed, wind the warp onto the back beam using cardboard or warp sticks between each layer of warp. If using a floor loom, it is easier if you have a helper to wind on while you hold the warp under tension. When about 30 in (76 cm) of the warp remains, insert the cross sticks in the cross and thread the warp through the heddles and the reed, then tie it onto the front beam, making sure the tension is even. The loom is now ready for weaving.

Dressing the loom from front to back

This method does not require a raddle. The cross sticks are inserted and the warp is first threaded through the reed, then the heddles, and tied onto the back beam. It is then wound onto the back beam under tension, inserting cardboard or warp sticks between each layer of warp. The warp is then tied onto the front beam and the loom is ready for weaving.

winding on to the back roller Showing sticks and cardboard between each layer of warp.

using a threading hook This tool assists in threading the warp ends though the heddle.

Balanced and unbalanced weaves

A weave can be balanced or unbalanced. Balanced weaves are those in which the number of weft threads per inch or centimetre is the same as the number of warp threads. In unbalanced weaves, the thread count per inch or centimetre differs for warp and weft.

Reeds and sleying

Looms are usually supplied with a 12-dent reed (that is, one that has 12 dents, or spaces, to the inch). In general use, one or two threads are passed through each dent of the reed, with perhaps double threads for a selvedge; however, a weaver should have reeds of different dentages for a variety of fabric weights. A second choice would probably be either ten or eight dents. A four-dent reed is suitable for rugs and can be used as a raddle.

To obtain the maximum value from any single reed, warps may be sleyed at one, two or three ends per dent, or alternating one end and two ends per dent. These methods of uneven denting will leave reeding marks in the woven fabric, particularly if the sley repeat does not divide into the weave repeat. For example, 2/2 twill has weave repeats on four ends and is best sleyed one, two or four per dent, not three per dent; mock leno has weave repeats on six ends and is best sleyed one or three per dent, not two or four.

Depending on the yarn and weave, reeding marks may disappear after the fabric is removed from the loom and washed, although they generally remain.

four-shaft double weave This is an example of a balanced weave.

dents A close-up of dents in the reed; the wooden frame that encloses the reed is the beater.

Weaving

Before weaving commences, the weaver must decide what type of shuttle to use. A stick shuttle works well for narrow weaving, but if weaving a wider piece a boat shuttle makes the weaving process much quicker and easier. If using a mohair or heavier yarn for the weft, a ski shuttle enables more yarn to be wound and is easy to throw across any width of weaving (see also page 10). If you are using two wefts, you will need two shuttles.

The weaving process may appear to be a mechanical sequence of actions — treadle depression, shed opening, weft insertion and beating — however, to weave a variety of cloth weights and qualities takes both skill and experience. A steady rhythm is essential for even weaving. The quality of a piece of handwoven cloth depends on the evenness of the tensions of the warp and weft threads. An even beat is very important and the weft should never be pulled tightly, but entered in the shed at a 45-degree angle. The weft is packed into place with the beater, the shed is changed and the process repeated. This simple operation can have many variations, each suitable for different types of weaving. The weaver may vary the moment at which he or she beats — sometimes it is better to change the shed, beat, throw the shuttle and beat again.

At the beginning and end of a piece, weave a header (several picks of plain weave) in a thicker yarn to draw the threads together. These threads prevent the cloth from unravelling when cut from the loom.

Joining in new weft threads

During the weaving, when the yarn on the bobbin or shuttle runs out, a new thread will need to be joined in. When starting a new bobbin of the same colour, you can overlap the new thead with the old weft for about 1 in (2.5 cm) in the same shed. If using a thick plied yarn, the old and new threads can be split so the overlapping area is not too thick. If using wool, often the new and old threads can be spliced together. If starting a new colour, finish the old colour by taking the yarn back on itself in the same shed at the selvedge for about 1 in (2.5 cm). The new colour is added in the same way.

header Two warp sticks are used as a header here instead of several picks of plain weave.

weft pick Pass the shuttle through the shed so that the weft enters at a 45-degree angle.

beating Beat the weft to pack it firmly into place.

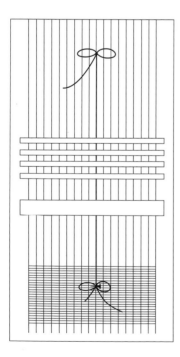

inspecting When you remove the cloth from the loom, check for skipped or broken threads, then repair them straight away. (Here, both the face and back of this eight-shaft deflected double weave fabric can be seen.)

diagram 1 Repairing broken warp threads
The new warp thread (shown in red) is tied onto the broken warp

Repairing errors

Should you notice an error while weaving, it is easiest to repair it while the web is still on the loom and under tension, but repairs can also be made once the fabric has been removed from the loom. A handy tool for mending is a yarn needle at least 5 in (12 cm) long, which can be used to weave in a replacement thread.

Skipped threads

Sometimes you may find that a thread, be it warp or weft, has been miswoven so that it skips over threads it wasn't supposed to. To fix it, thread the needle with a new piece of the same yarn and stitch it into the fabric where it was supposed to go, following the correct thread order and stitching along the line of the original thread. Extend the stitching for a little way past the error on both sides, then cut the thread close to the fabric. When the cloth is cut from the loom, cut away the erroneous part of the original thread close to the fabric. The overlapping area of the new and old threads will keep the repair secure; washing the fabric afterwards will help secure the threads further.

Repairing broken warp threads

Sometimes during the weaving, a warp thread breaks. This must be repaired before continuing with the weaving. Take about 1 yard (1 m) of the same yarn, pass one end through the appropriate place in the reed and the heddle to the back of the loom where it can be tensioned over the back of the loom, attached to, say, a cotton reel, or tied with a bow to the other end of the broken thread. Attach a dressmaker's pin to the woven cloth about 1 in (2.5 cm) from the fell and wind the other end of the new warp around the pin (see Diagram 1). After about 12 in (30 cm) of weaving, when the new warp becomes part of the cloth, the pin can be removed. The broken thread should now be long enough to attach to the weaving, fastened around a pin in the same way as before. Loose ends can be darned into the weaving when the cloth is removed from the loom.

Glossary

Apron Length of firm cloth (or cords) attached to the warp and cloth beams, to which sticks are attached. The warp ends are tied to the sticks. The apron allows the ends of the warp to be brought closer to the shafts.

Balanced weave A weave in which the number of warp threads per inch or per centimetre is equal to the number of weft threads per inch or per centimetre.

Batten See Beater.

Beam

  Back beam The bar at the back of the loom over which the warp runs from the warp beam roller to the shafts.

  Breast beam (or **front beam**) The bar at the front of the loom over which the cloth runs to the cloth beam roller.

  Cloth beam The roller at the front of the loom on which the woven cloth is wound.

  Warp beam The roller at the back of the loom on which the warp is wound.

Beaming (or rolling on) The process of winding the warp onto the warp beam.

Beater (or batten) A frame that swings on the loom framework. The beater holds the reed and packs the weft into place.

Bobbin A spool onto which thread is wound for weaving.

Bobbin winder A manual or electric tool for winding yarn onto a bobbin or spool.

Brake A mechanism on the warp beam and the cloth beam that prevents them from turning. When engaged, the brake holds the warp under tension; it is released to allow to warp to advance.

Butterfly A package of yarn for weft which is wound on the hand, between thumb and little finger, in a figure-of-eight fashion.

Castle Structure across the top of a loom from which the shafts are hung.

Chaining A process of looping the warp upon itself (see page 13) to prevent it from tangling while it is transferred from the warping board to the loom.

Cone A package of yarn wound on a conical cardboard shape.

Cop A package of yarn wound on a cylindrical tube.

Count The size of yarn in the indirect system (see also page 23).

Cross (or lease) The point at which the warp threads meet each other coming and going around the pegs on the warping board. This prevents tangling and aids in the threading of the ends through the heddles in their correct order.

Cross sticks (or lease sticks) A pair of smooth sticks with a hole in each end so they can be tied together; they are placed through the cross to secure and maintain it.

Cross ties Temporary ties applied to the warp when it is on the warping board; used to maintain the cross until the cross sticks are inserted.

Dent The space between two wires in a reed. The sett of reeds is gauged by the number of dents (or splits) per inch or centimetre.

cross The point at which the warp ends meet when winding the warp on a warping board.

treadles and lamms on a floor loom

Design Diagram of cloth structure obtained by combining the threading draft and the lifting plan (see also pages 24–25).

Direct system A means of measuring the size of yarn (see also page 23).

Draft A graph that indicates the order in which the ends are drawn through the heddles on the shafts.

Drawing-in See Threading.

Dressing a loom All the processes of preparing a loom for weaving.

E/cm Ends per centimetre.

End A single warp thread. The term refers to the entire length of the thread, not just the actual end of it.

End and end Alternating single ends of warp in two colours.

Epi Ends per inch.

Fell The fell line of the cloth is the front or forward edge of the weaving, or the point where the last weft pick has been inserted.

Filling Another term for the weft.

Finishing Work done on cloth after it has been removed from the loom, for example washing, hem stitching or pressing.

Float An end or pick that goes over or under two or more warp ends or two or more picks; for example in a twill weave, the weft goes over and under two warp threads.

Floating selvedge A warp end at either side of the warp which is not threaded through a heddle eye, but is sleyed through the reed.

Grey cloth Cloth in its loom state prior to finishing.

Guide string A preliminary measuring thread used to determine the correct warp length and the pattern of winding on the warping board; see also page 12.

Harness Another name for a shaft; used more in America than elsewhere.

Header Picks woven at the beginning of the warp to test its threading and tension.

Heddles Strings or wires suspended between the shafts, with eyes through which the warp ends are threaded.

Indirect system A means of measuring the size of yarn (see also page 23).

Lamms Horizontal pieces positioned between the treadles and shafts.

Lease See Cross.

Lease sticks (rods) See Cross sticks.

Lifting plan (peg or pegging plan) A plan showing the order in which the shafts are to be operated.

Loom waste The unweavable portion of the warp threads that are required for tying on to the loom, and which are cut off at the end of the weaving process.

Over-dyeing The process of dyeing a second colour over a previous one.

P/cm Picks per centimetre.

Peg (or pegging) plan See Lifting plan.

Pick A single pass of weft. Also known as a shot or filling.

Pick and pick Alternating single picks of weft in two colours.

shafts, warp threads and heddles

Pick-up stick A smooth stick with a pointed end; used to pick up selected warp ends.

Plain weave (or tabby) A basic weave of one up and one down in both the warp and the weft.

Ppi Picks per inch.

Raddle A frame (often with a removable cap on top), having pegs set at equal intervals; used for spreading the warp to its correct width when beaming.

Reed A comb-like frame composed of thin metal slats, which is used for spacing the warp ends and beating in the weft. The reed is held in place by the beater.

Reed hook (or sley hook) A thin, flat, S-shaped hook used for sleying the reed.

Rolling on See Beaming.

Selvedge The point at which the weft binds the warp to form a firmly woven closed edge on each side of the cloth. It may consist of only one thread, or several.

Sett The number of warp threads (or ends) per inch or per centimetre as determined by the yarn thickness and the particular end use. Spelled 'set' when used as a verb and 'sett' when used as a noun.

Shaft (or harness) A unit composed of heddles and heddle bars or frames.

Shed The opening between the layers of warp threads; made by raising or lowering one or more, but not all, of the shafts. The loaded shuttle is passed through the shed when weaving in order to deposit the weft thread, or pick.

Shot One pick of weft (or filling).

Shuttle A tool on which the weft yarn is wound so it can be passed through the shed.

Sley hook See Threading hook.

Sleying The threading of the warp ends through the dents of the reed.

Tabby Another term for plain weave.

Temple (tenterhook) An implement used for preventing the selvedges pulling in too much. Placed on the woven cloth in front of the reed.

Tex The size of a yarn in the direct system (see also page 23).

Threading (drawing in) The threading of the warp ends through the eyes of the heddles according to the draft.

Threading hook Used for threading the warp ends through the eyes of the heddles.

Tie-up Instructions for a floor loom — how the shafts are to be tied so that a foot pedal operates them.

Treadling plan The order in which the treadles of a floor loom are to be operated. The treadling plan, tie-up and threading draft combine to produce the design or draw-down.

Warp The threads running the length of the loom, which are held under tension. These run lengthwise in the woven cloth.

Warping board A board or frame set with pegs which is used for winding the warp.

Web A piece of woven fabric.

Weft The thread carried by the shuttle which is passed through the shed to interlace with the warp ends. These run widthwise in the woven cloth.

shed in warp The space between the lifted and lowered warp threads is known as the shed. It is through this space that the shuttle is passed, or 'thrown'.

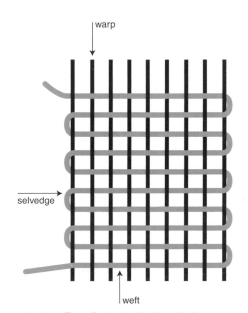

selvedge The selvedge is the closed edge of the fabric, and the point at which the weft threads wrap around the warp.

Yarn calculation

Calculation for the warp is the width of the weaving multiplied by the ends per inch or per centimetre multiplied by the length of the warp. (Work in metric or imperial; don't mix the two.) For example:

If working in inches: For a warp 24 inches wide, sett 10 epi, length 72 inches:
24 x 10 x 72 = 17,280.

Divide the result by 36 inches to give the number of yards needed:

17,280 ÷ 36 = 480 yards.

If working in centimetres: For a warp 60 cm wide, sett 5 e/cm, length 200 cm:
60 x 5 x 200 = 60,000.

Divide the result by 100 cm to give the number of metres needed for the warp:

60,000 ÷ 100 = 600 metres.

Calculation for the weft is the width of the weaving multiplied by the picks per inch or per cm multiplied by the length of the weaving. For example:

If working in inches: For a weft 20 inches wide, 10 picks per inch, length 36 inches:
20 x 10 x 36 = 7,200 inches.

Divide the result by 36 to give the number of yards required for the weft:

7,200 ÷ 36 = 200 yards.

If working in centimetres: For a weft 50 cm wide, 4 picks per cm, length 200 cm: 50 x 4 x 200 = 40,000.

Divide the result by 100 to give the number of metres required for the weft:

40,000 ÷ 100 = 400 metres.

Yarns

A warp yarn can be composed of any fibre so long as it can sustain both considerable tension during weaving and the friction caused by the movement of the shafts and the reed. The yarn needs to be chosen for its strength, elasticity and abrasion resistance.

Weft yarns are not subject to the same strain or abrasion and therefore almost any type of yarn can be used. The weft yarn does not have to be the same type of yarn as the warp; for instance, a soft wool yarn can be used with a cotton warp. Avoid highly twisted yarns, as they do not pack down well in the weaving and can distort the weave. They can be used for special effects by experienced weavers, but are best not used by beginners.

Try a weft of the same or an analogous colour or texture (white and cream used together for warp and weft are very effective), or mix textures — for example, shiny and dull, rough and smooth, dull and metallic.

Pulling in can occur if the weft is pulled too tightly, thus forcing the cloth out of shape. Also, the reed may wear the selvedge threads. Be careful of the non-elasticity of some fancy yarns, as often the pulling in is not apparent until too late.

warp yarns These should be chosen for their strength and abrasion resistance.

weft yarns Fancy and textured yarns, as well as plain, can be used for the weft.

Count system

The count system refers to the measurement of the thickness of yarns. There are two systems, direct and indirect.

Indirect

This Imperial system is very complicated, as yardages vary for different types of yarn. The unit length of 1s count (that is, one unit length to 1 lb weight) varies with different fibres and different spinning systems, for example:

Woollen spun Galashiels	cut	200 yards
Yorkshire	skein	256 yards
West of England	hank	320 yards
Worsted	hank	560 yards
Linen	lea	300 yards
Cotton	hank	840 yards
Spun silk	hank	840 yards

When a yarn in any of the above systems is plied — that is, when two yarns of identical count are twisted together — the yarn is twice as thick and the length of a pound weight is halved. For example, with 2/8s cotton, the length of this yarn would be 8 x 840 ÷ 2 = 3360 yards. Fortunately today most yarns have the yardage noted on the package, which makes calculation for your weaving much easier.

Direct

The direct, or Tex, system is based on a fixed-length system, that is, weight per unit length. The Tex count is a metric system, and represents the weight in grams per kilometre of yarn. For example, a yarn numbered 10 Tex measures 1 kilometre and weighs 10 grams. The Tex number increases with the size of the yarn. The term 'folded' is used in preference to 'plied' yarn when two or more yarns are twisted together, and the direction of the twist is included in the information. For example, 20 Tex/2S indicates that two threads of 10 Tex are folded in an 'S' direction. The resultant count will be 20 Tex because the weight is exactly doubled. It is hoped that this system will be adopted universally as it is much easier and applies to all yarns.

Sett

A quick way of working out the sett of a yarn is to wind the yarn around a ruler over 1 inch (2.5 cm) so that the threads just touch each other. When the warp and weft are of the same yarn, the sett will be half the number of threads that wind to 1 inch (2.5 cm) for plain weave. Add about a third more ends for twill. When calculating the amount of warp yarn needed, allowances must be made for tie-ups at the front and back of the loom, take-up of yarn when weaving, and shrinkage. On a floor loom, allow an extra yard or metre — on a table loom, half a yard or half a metre is usually all that is needed.

The weft usually takes about three quarters as much yarn as the warp, as you don't have to allow for warp take-up and tying on. It is always better to be generous when calculating how much yarn is needed. See opposite for more detail on yarn calculation.

testing sett Winding the yarn around a ruler will help you to calculate its sett.

Reading drafts in handweaving

A 'draw down' — sometimes known as a 'comprehensive draft' — gives a picture of the three components of pattern making on a loom: the threading draft, the lifting plan and the design resulting from a combination of these two.

In threading, the warp threads are drawn through the heddles in a pre-determined sequence; changes in this sequence alter the resultant pattern. The simplest threading is the straight (or twill) threading. On a four-shaft loom, the first warp thread is drawn through the first heddle on shaft 1; the second warp end through the first heddle on shaft 2; the third warp end through the first heddle on shaft 3; the fourth warp end through the first heddle on shaft 4; the fifth warp end on the second heddle on shaft 1; the sixth warp end on the second heddle of shaft 2, and so on. This is continued across the width of the loom — on an eight-shaft loom, the same sequence is followed through to the eighth shaft.

The symbols used to represent drafts vary between publications, but the principles remain the same. The simplest and least confusing method is to use numbers referring to the number of the shaft on which that end is threaded, written on squared paper so that each vertical space represents a warp thread; see Diagram 1.

If you read from left to right, then thread from left to right. If you read from right to left, thread from right to left. On a balanced weave, it makes no difference in which direction you thread; if there is a different pattern at one end, then it would just be reversed. A lifting plan relates directly to the draft, and shows the order in which the shafts are lifted after they have been threaded. This is written on squared paper with crosses (see Diagram 2) to indicate a lift of warp over weft. A lifting plan also uses each vertical row to represent a warp thread — a horizontal row refers to one pick.

Straight draft   Fancy draft

diagram 1 Threading draft Shown for both a straight and a fancy weave

Drafts, lifting plans and designs

A lifting plan is read from the bottom up, as shown in Diagram 2. By looking at each vertical row in the lifting plan in turn, the action of each warp thread can be seen. For example:

Thread number 1: lifts, falls, lifts, falls
Thread number 2: falls, lifts, lifts, falls
Thread number 3: lifts, falls, falls, lifts
Thread number 4: falls, lifts, falls, lifts

A lifting plan can only be as wide, or over as many ends, as there are shafts threaded. For example, on a four-shaft loom, the lifting plan will be four ends wide. However, it can be as long, or over as many picks, as required.

A design is a combination of these two. With a straight draft, the design and lifting plan will be the same, but any variation in the threading will produce a different design. The design will be as long as the lifting plan and as wide as the draft; see Diagram 3.

When using a floor loom, the same rules apply, except now you have a draft, tie-up and treadling plan. The tie-up shows how the shafts are tied to the treadles. The draft is read from right to left and the treadling plan is read from top to bottom. It works the same as for a table loom, except with a floor loom the treadles lift the shafts; see Diagram 4.

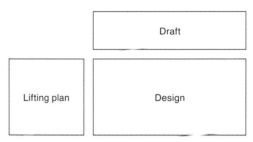

				Pick	Shafts
		X	X	4	3 and 4
X	X			3	1 and 2
	X		X	2	2 and 4
X		X		1	1 and 3

diagram 2 Lifting plan

Draft	
Lifting plan	**Design**

diagram 3 Design with draft and lifting plan for a table loom

Draft	Tie up
Design	Treadling plan

diagram 4 Design with draft, tie-up and treadling plan for a floor loom

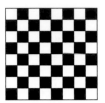

diagram 1 Plain weave

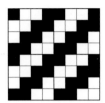

diagram 2 Twill weave, with twill lines running from left to right

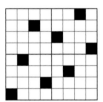

diagram 3 Satin weave

rosepath An example of a Rosepath boundweave on four shafts.

The basic weaves

Plain weave

Plain weave (also called tabby; see Diagram 1) is the simplest and most important of all weave structures. Each warp interlaces with each weft in an alternating fashion, making the weave very strong and the material somewhat stiff. This weave can be woven on any number of shafts.

Twill weave

Twill is a versatile weave that possesses nearly unlimited possibilities for variation. The structure of twills is based on the overlapping and staggering of warp and weft threads to produce diagonal lines (see Diagram 2). Twill lines may run from left to right or right to left.

Satin weave

Satin weaves form an unbroken cloth surface, the thread intersections being hidden as far as possible (see Diagram 3). This weave makes a single-sided cloth and has an unbalanced warp-to-weft ratio. If the weave has a warp surface, it is called satin; if there is a weft preponderance, it is known as sateen. The weave notation is usually given as a sateen weave to save time. Satin weaves are frequently woven face down to keep the number of shafts to be lifted to a minimum. This weave needs very fine and close settings of the warp and is rarely satisfactory for the handweaver.

Rosepath

There are innumerable types of weaves possible, ranging widely in complexity. The Rosepath threading is popular among modern weavers interested in texture weaving. It is sometimes used for dress fabrics and upholsteries in its all-over form, but it is more often used to weave attractive borders for placemats, skirts, stoles, curtains and similar items. It can also be used as a bound weave suitable for rugs. The Rosepath threading, an eight-thread point twill, enables the weaver to weave a number of different designs on the same warp. It is one if the most widely employed drafts, and has been used for hundreds of years in the Scandinavian countries, where is it known as Rosengang. There are several methods of weaving Rosepath and endless variations of lifting to produce the patterns. Experienced weavers claim there are still many unrecorded lifting plans.

Popular Rosepath weaves

A weave with a 2/2 twill produces horizontal zig-zag lines (see Diagram 4). When woven as drawn in, a 2/2 twill or 1/3 twill produces a diamond design (see Diagrams 5 and 6). 'Woven as drawn in' means that the weft picks follow the same order as the draft. (When using a 1/3 twill, 3/1 will show on the reverse.)

Other variations

The diamond design can be enlarged by weaving as drawn in or with a reverse twill and repeating each pick. If a pick is repeated, a plain-weave binder must be used between every 2/2 twill pick. Use an extra shuttle for the plain-weave binder, which should be a similar colour to the warp but finer (sewing thread can be used.) Both pattern and plain weave picks go in the same direction — plain weave 1–3 from right to left, and 2–4 from left to right. Keep the same continuity of pattern and binder throughout.

Border designs can be planned by selecting part of the pattern and repeating the same pick several times. It is not necessary to use a plain-weave binder when the lifting follows twill; however, when the same pick is repeated, it must be used.

The designs may be planned on graph paper; however, the lifts of 1–3 and 2–4 must be kept for plain weave only. Use 2/2, 1/3 or 3/1 lifts for the pattern.

Note that in drafting these designs you are marking the warps up — if you weave the design in this way, the blanks on the graph paper will show as the coloured weft on the faces of the woven fabric and the marks will show as the warp. The marks you have designed on the graph will show as the weft floats on the back of the fabric. To reverse this result, it will be necessary to lift the unmarked squares.

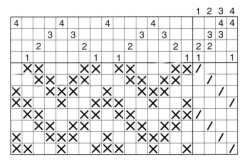

diagram 4 2/2 twill forming a zigzag pattern

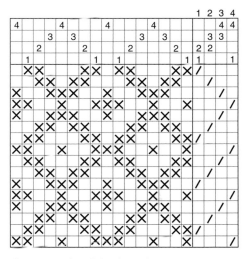

diagram 5 2/2 twill forming a diamond pattern

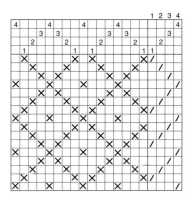

diagram 6 1/3 twill forming a diamond pattern

Hem stitching

Hem stitching is an optional finish that serves both decorative and practical purposes. It prevents the weft from unravelling when the weaving is taken off the loom, which can otherwise be a problem with scarves and wraps (although it does not matter when weaving a length of fabric that will later be made into a garment). Most weavers use hem stitching when they want to leave a fringe; this is mainly on scarves and wraps but can also be used for garments.

If intending to hem stitch, weave three or four rows of plain weave, ending with the shuttle on the right if you are right-handed or on the left if you are left-handed. Leave a length of weft yarn three times the width of the weaving; use this to work the hem stitching. Do the hem stitching while the weaving is still on the loom, following Diagram 1. The thread is passed under a group of warp ends above the fell, brought up and back to starting point, encircling the group of ends. It is then passed under the same group of ends and brought out through 2 or 3 picks from the fell line. This process is repeated across the warp.

Finishes for woven cloth

The appearance and handle — that is, the feel or touch — of many fabrics do not develop fully until the fabric has been washed. If you wish to hem stitch the fabric (see left), it is easiest to do so before it is removed from the loom. Every woven fabric should be carefully inspected as soon as it is taken off the loom, and all broken ends and weaving faults repaired straight away (see page 18). If you want to make a fringe, make sure when cutting the weaving from the loom that you leave warp ends that are long enough for the purpose. If the weaving has not been hem stitched, secure each end by overlocking it or using a machine zigzag stitch. The fabric is then ready to be washed.

Washing

The method of washing will depend on the end use of the fabric. Wraps and scarves can be hand washed (if the fabric is wool, use an approved wool detergent), rinsed well, put through the spin cycle of the washing machine, steam pressed and then hung to dry. When dry, steam press again. Fabric lengths that are intended for use in garments can be hand washed as above, or put through the gentle cycle in the washing machine, and then the above steps followed. It is not necessary to wash floor rugs.

Blanket stitch

Blanket stitch is another way of finishing off the edge of the garment, and can be used on either a selvedge edge or an overlocked edge (see Diagram 2). It is also used to reinforce an edge, for example to reinforce the end of the seam at the neck edge of a garment such as the Reversible Poncho (see page 55). Choose a toning or contrasting yarn depending on the desired effect.

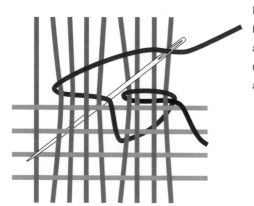

diagram 1 Hem stitching

Woven seam

A woven seam is only used when joining two selvedges together, and saves using a sewing machine. It is started and finished the same way in which you would join any two pieces of fabric together, and is worked by bringing the needle from back to front on alternate edges (see Diagram 3). Use a yarn that blends into the background. Avoid using a yarn that breaks easily, or a fancy or highly textured yarn, as this will be difficult to pull through the fabric. For a woven seam, it is usually best to use the weft yarn used for the weaving.

Twisted fringe

Divide the number of strands for each fringe into two groups. Twist each group clockwise until it kinks. Bring both the groups together and allow them to twist around each other in the opposite direction. Secure the ends with an overhand knot to prevent untwisting.

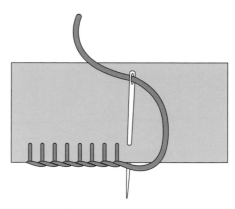

diagram 2 Blanket stitch Insert the needle from front to back, bringing it out at the edge of the fabric. Pass it in front of the yarn and pull the yarn until it is firm. Repeat as required. The stitches can be short or long, and widely or narrowly spaced, depending on the effect required and the looseness of the weave. If being used as reinforcement on loosely woven cloth, closer blanket stitches are more effective.

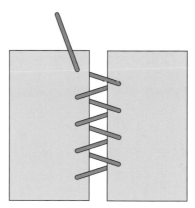

diagram 3 Woven seam Bring the needle from back to front on alternate edges.

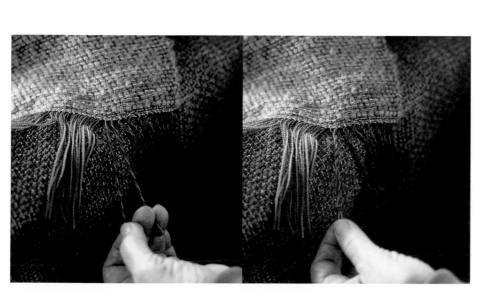

twisted fringe, step one Twist two groups of threads in the same direction.

twisted fringe, step two Allow the two groups to twist together, then knot the end to secure.

Weaving on a small loom

When weaving on a small loom, three successive layers of yarn are laid down by winding the yarn around the nails on the frame. After threading the yarn into a long needle, the fourth and final layer is woven through the other layers. An even tension should be maintained throughout; if it is too tight, the square will shrink when removed from the loom. The following are general directions for weaving with small looms; any loom that you buy will come with its own instructions, which may differ slightly from those that follow.

First layer

The starting corner of the loom is marked with a drawing pin. Hold the loom with this corner facing you and at the lower left. Leaving a tail of about 6 in (15 cm), wind the yarn around the drawing pin to secure it. Take the yarn to the far side of the loom, passing it to the left of the first pin on each end (see Diagram 1). On the far side of the loom, pass the yarn to the right, around the first two pins. Return to the side nearest you, taking the yarn between the second and third pins of the first group. Pass the yarn to the right around the next two pins, then across to the far side of the loom, and between the first and second pins in the group directlly across. Continue in this manner, passing the yarn between the first and second pins in each group on each side then around two pins to the right, until you have reached the lower right-hand corner and the yarn emerges where Indicated, between the last two pins of the bottom row.

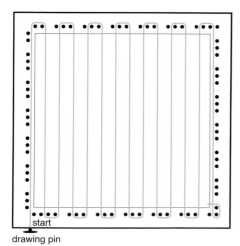

drawing pin

diagram 1 First layer Starting at the bottom left corner, pass the yarn back and forth as indicated, going around two pins at a time.

Second layer

Pass the yarn around the first two pins on the right and across to the left side, bringing the yarn out between the first and second pins of the first group (see Diagram 2). Continue as for the first layer, until you reach the right side of the loom and the yarn emerges between the last two pins of the top row of that side.

Third layer

Pass the yarn between the first two pins on the right-hand side, across to the left side, and around the middle two pins. Then go across to the far side, bringing the yarn out in the space between two groups of pins. Go around two pins to the right and back to the near side, again coming out in the wide space between two groups of pins. Continue thus until the yarn emerges in the space between the two pins at the lower right-hand corner.

Fourth layer

For the fourth layer, the yarn is threaded into a long needle with an upturned tip and is woven under and over the strands of the other layers (see Diagram 4). The amount of yarn required for this final layer will depend on the size of your loom and the thickness of the yarn, and will be stated in your loom's instructions. Measure off the correct amount and thread it into the needle. Starting at the lower right,

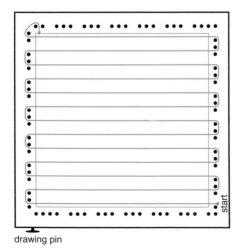

diagram 2 **Second layer** This is laid down at right angles to the first layer.

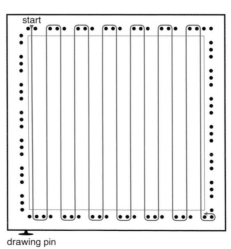

diagram 3 **Third layer** Laid down parallel to the first layer and at right angles to the second.

diagram 4 **Fourth layer** Using a needle, the fourth layer is woven through the strands of the previous layers.

insert the tip of the needle over the outside loop of yarn between the pins, then under the first strand, over the second, under the third, and so on, continuing across the row. When weaving this layer, it is important to turn the needle to raise and lower the bent tip to go over and under the strands. If you employ a normal sewing action — that is, raising then lowering the threaded end of the needle — the strands will be lifted off the pins.

At the end of the first woven row, the yarn emerges in the space below the first group of pins on the left side. Pull the yarn completely through, taking care not to pull too tightly, or the finished square will be uneven. Insert the needle between the second and third pins from the bottom left. Weaving from left to right, take the needle over the loop of yarn between the pins, under the first strand, over the second, under the third, and so on. The rows of this layer lie parallel to, but between, the strands of the second layer.

At the end of the second woven row, the yarn will emerge in the first wide space at the lower right of the loom. Pull the yarn completely through. Going around two pins each time and working between the strands of the second layer, continue weaving the rows. The last row is woven just below the top row of pins and the yarn emerges at the top right of the loom.

Finishing

To finish, turn the corner and tie the yarn into the first loop around the pins. Before removing the square from the loom, check that the strands of yarn are straight and that the outside strand on each side lies snugly against the row of pins. Any irregularities may be straightened out by stroking the fabric with the needle.

The square can now be carefully removed from the loom, using the needle to lift the loops over the pin heads. Once two adjacent sides have been removed, the square will lift off easily.

The look of the squares can be varied in several ways: by using different weights of yarn; by winding with one colour and weaving with another; or by winding and weaving with two strands of a lightweight yarn. The finished squares can be sewn together using the tails of yarn left at the beginning and end of the squares, or they can be crocheted together as in the projects on pages 82 and 102.

joining small-loom squares Small-loom squares can be sewn together, or, as in this detail of the Triangular shawl (see page 102) crocheted together for a decorative effect.

Wool and mohair wrap

This cosy wrap in heather tones uses a combination of wool and mohair yarns for a luxurious effect.

The basketweave blocks among the plain weave result in an almost embossed effect.

Size 20 x 84 in (50 x 214 cm)

Equipment Eight-shaft loom, 24 in (60 cm) weaving width, ski shuttle

Techniques Basket weave and plain weave

Warp and weft yarns 4½ oz (125 g) space-dyed blue-black bouclé mohair, 4½ oz (125 g) 3-ply green wool, 1 oz (25 g) 2-ply dark grey mohair, 4½ oz (125 g) 6-ply fuzzy taupe mohair, 1 oz (25 g) 2-ply mauve mohair

Reed 10 dents per in (2.5 cm)

Sett 12 ends per in (2.5 cm). Sley 1 green wool and 1 dark grey mohair together

Selvedge 3 ends per dent twice on each side

Width in reed 24 in (60 cm)

Finished width 22 in (55 cm)

Weft sett 12 picks per in (2.5 cm)

Number of ends 328

Warp length 120 in (305 cm), which includes ties, loom waste and take-up

Designer Helen Frostell

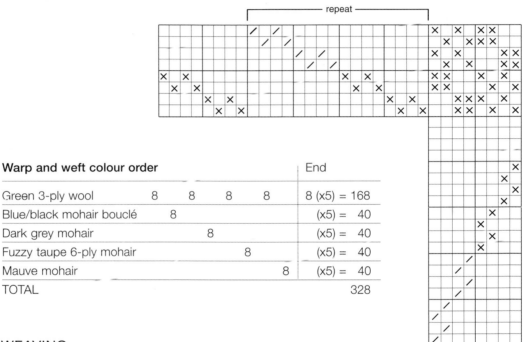

Warp and weft colour order					End	
Green 3-ply wool	8	8	8	8	8 (x5) =	168
Blue/black mohair bouclé	8				(x5) =	40
Dark grey mohair		8			(x5) =	40
Fuzzy taupe 6-ply mohair			8		(x5) =	40
Mauve mohair				8	(x5) =	40
TOTAL						328

X green
/ mohair
follow warp colour order

WEAVING

As mohair tends to stick, this can be overcome by opening the following shed while the beater is still at the fell line. Leave 8 in (20 cm) of warp at each end for fringing. Weave a header at both ends to hold weave firmly.

FINISHING

Remove from loom. Make a twisted fringe (see page 29) with about five threads in each hand. Twist to the right, then let the two cords twist back around each other in the opposite direction. Finish with an overhand knot. Hand-wash in warm, soapy water and agitate firmly. Rinse. Spin dry for 10 seconds. Roll firmly around a large tube for 24 hours, then dry flat. Trim fringes.

Three lace scarves from the same warp

Making more than one item from the same warp reduces the time needed for the lengthy process of warping. Each of these three delicately patterned scarves uses a different three-end huck lace design. A natural mulberry silk yarn is used here, but the weave patterns could easily be adapted for thicker yarns or, equally well, for larger garments.

Size of each scarf 7 x 73 in (18 x 185 cm)

Equipment Eight-shaft loom, throw shuttle

Technique Three-end huck lace

Warp and weft yarn For three scarves: 10½ oz (300 g) 20/2 mulberry silk. Add 3½ oz (100 g) for any additional scarves

Reed 10 dents per in (2.5 cm)

Sett 20 ends per in (2.5 cm). Sley 2 ends per dent

Width in reed 8 in (20 cm)

Weft sett 20 picks per in (2.5 cm)

Warp length 8¼ yds (7.5 m); add 2⅔ yds (2.4 m) for any additional scarves

Number of ends 163

Designer Mary Hawkins

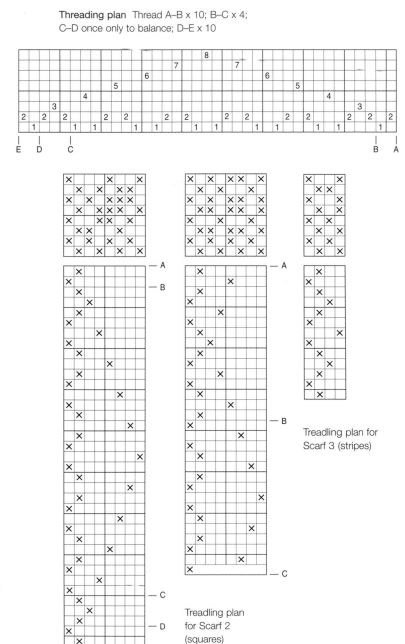

Treadling plan for
Scarf 1 (diamonds)

Treadling plan
for Scarf 2
(squares)

Treadling plan for
Scarf 3 (stripes)

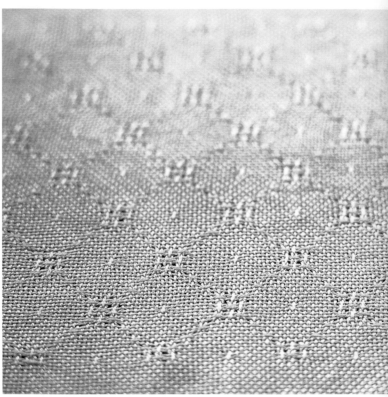

scarf 1 Diamonds and lace squares

THREADING

Thread from A–B 10 times (for plain weave
border); from B–C four times (pattern
repeats); from C–D once only (to balance
pattern); and from D–E 10 times (for
remaining border).

SCARF 1: DIAMONDS

Allow 7 in (18 cm) for the fringe (part of
this can come out of the tie-on). Weave A–B
(plain weave)for 2 in (5 cm), then follow
treadling plan 1; weave B–C for 75 in
(1.9 m), ending with C–D once only to
balance the design. Weave 2 in (5 cm) plain
weave. Allow 7 in (18 cm) fringe for Scarf 1,
then 7 in (18 cm) fringe for Scarf 2.

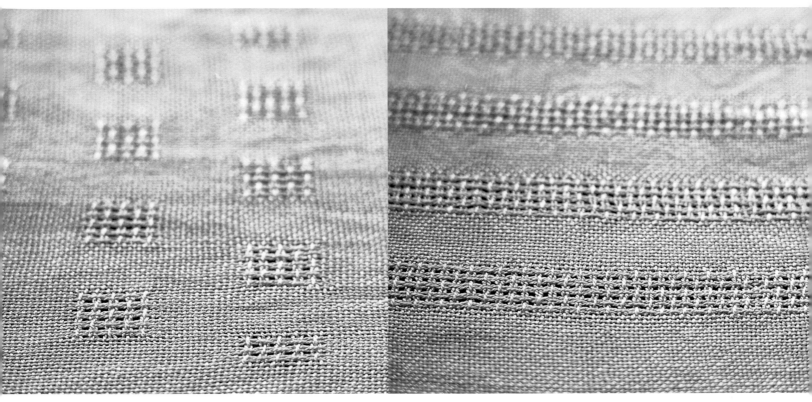

scarf 2 Lace squares

scarf 3 Lace stripes

SCARF 2: SQUARES

Weave 2 in (5 cm) of plain weave, as for
Scarf 1, then follow treadling plan 2 for
A–B, then 15 picks plain weave, then B–C
as per treadling plan, then 15 picks plain
weave. Continue thus for 75 in (1.9 m).
Weave 2 in (5 cm) plain weave. Allow 7 in
(18 cm) fringe for Scarf 2, then 7 in (18 cm)
fringe for Scarf 3.

SCARF 3: STRIPES

Weave 2 in (5 cm) of plain weave, as for
Scarf 1, then follow treadling plan 3 for 75 in
(1.9 m). Weave 2 in (5 cm) plain weave.
Allow 7 in (18 cm) fringe.

Remove the fabric from the loom. Cut the
three scarves apart.

FINISHING

Finish each scarf with a twisted fringe (see
page 29). Wash in wool-approved detergent
and rinse in fabric conditioner. Roll in a
towel to remove excess moisture (do not
wring). Dry flat in shade. When almost dry,
iron to complete the drying process.

Furoshiki bag

Furoshiki is a Japanese word meaning 'wrapper'. This bag is simply but ingeniously constructed from a folded rectangle woven of strips of kimono material on a cotton warp.

Size 17 in (43 cm) square, not including handle

Equipment Four-shaft loom, with 16 in (40 cm) weaving width, ski shuttle, throw shuttle

Technique Plain weave

Warp yarn Black 16/2 cotton

Weft yarn Kimono fabric cut into ½ in (12 mm) strips with the grain, and black 16/2 cotton

Reed 12 dents per in (2.5 cm)

Sett 12 ends per in (2.5 cm)

Selvedge 2 ends twice in each heddle on each side. Use floating selvedge

Width in reed 16 in (40 cm)

Finished width 13½ in (34 cm)

Weft sett 8 picks fabric strips plus 8 picks cotton per in (2.5 cm)

Warp length 75 in (190 cm), which includes 10 per cent shrinkage, ties, take-up and loom waste

Number of ends 200

Designer Helen Frostell

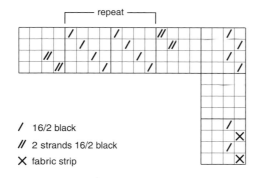

/   16/2 black
// 2 strands 16/2 black
X   fabric strip

WEAVING AND FINISHING

Weave a ½ in (12 mm) seam allowance with doubled 16/2 cotton. Then weave the bag, alternating 1 pick of fabric and 1 pick of 16/2 cotton. Weave so that the length is three times the width, taking shrinkage, take-up and seams into reckoning. Finish with a ½ in (12 mm) seam allowance. Secure the weave with some picks of cotton. Remove the fabric from the loom and machine zigzag each end to prevent fraying. Gently hand-wash. Press.

ASSEMBLY

Start with a rectangle of fabric three times as long as it is wide. Fold and sew the fabric following the diagram, A to A and B to B. Then pull up the two corners C and the shape will change.

For the handle, cut two strips of kimono fabric 13 x 1½ in (33 x 4 cm), or length and width desired. Having right sides together and raw edges even, and allowing a 1/4 in (6 mm) seam allowance, sew along both long sides and one short end. Turn through, press and attach to corners. Top stitch edges of handle. Bind the seams, or line the bag if desired.

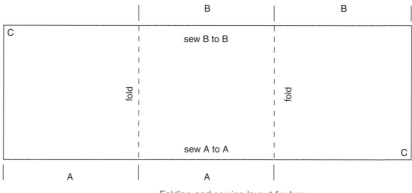

Folding and sewing layout for bag

Bouclé mohair wrap

This autumn-toned wrap is woven in bouclé mohair yarn and a fine 2/20 wool. Combining the bouclé with two picks of 2/20 wool in between each bouclé pick creates a lighter fabric.

Size 22 x 72 in (55 x 182 cm)

Equipment Four-shaft loom, with 24 in (60 cm) weaving width, ski shuttle, throw shuttle

Technique Plain weave and 1/3 twill

Warp yarn Bendigo Woollen Mills 2-ply pure wool, 336 yds (307 m) of each of three colours to match the mohair weft yarn

Weft yarn Touch Yarns (New Zealand) variegated bouclé mohair, 304 yds (278 m); and olive green 2/20s pure wool, 610 yds (558 m)

Reed 12 dents per in (2.5 cm)

Sett 12 ends per in (2.5 cm)

Selvedge Double thread through heddle at each end

Width in reed 24 in (60 cm)

Finished width of fabric 22 x 72 in (55 x 182 cm)

Weft sett 18 picks per in (2.5 cm): six picks bouclé yarn and 12 picks fine yarn

Warp length 3½ yds (3.2 m)

Number of ends 288

Designer Wendy Cartwright

WINDING THE WARP

Wind a warp in the 2-ply Bendigo wool from Bendigo using the three colours; these can be wound together with a finger between each thread to prevent tangling. The three ends can be taken through the cross together and threaded through the reed in the order preferred.

WEAVING

Use a ski shuttle for the mohair yarn and a throw shuttle for the fine yarn. Start the weaving with four plain-weave picks of the 2/20s wool, then weave one pick of bouclé and two picks of 2/20s yarn. Weave for approximately 76 in (193 cm), leaving 5 in (13 cm) of warp at each end for a fringe, and hem stitching each end while the fabric is still on the loom.

End the weaving with four plain-weave picks in the 2/20s wool; these extra four picks at each end make the hem stitching easier.

The finished size will be 22 x 72 in (55 x 182 cm); always measure on the loom without tension. Some length and width are always lost in the finishing process.

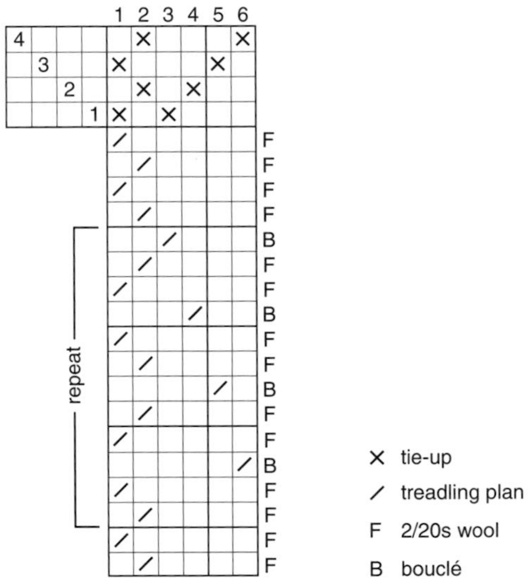

1 2 3 4 5 6
4
3
2
1
F
F
F
F
B
F
F
B
F
F
B
F
F
B
F
F
F
F
repeat
× tie-up
⁄ treadling plan
F 2/20s wool
B bouclé

FINISHING

Cut the wrap from the loom and twist the ends of the fringe (see page 29) before washing. Wash in a wool-approved detergent, then put through the spin cycle on a washing machine and steam press. Line dry and steam press again.

Monk's belt mat

Two subtly contrasting tones of linen are used here to form a striped band at either end of the weaving.

Size 17 x 12 in (43 x 30 cm)

Equipment Four-shaft loom with 13 in (33 cm) weaving width, throw shuttle

Technique Plain weave with monk's belt adaption

Warp yarn Unbleached linen 16/1, two ends used as one

Weft yarn Unbleached linen 16/1, and coloured linen 16/2 for the pattern

Reed 12 dents per in (2.5 cm)

Sett 24 ends per in (2.5 cm), using 2 ends as one

Selvedge 4 ends per heddle twice on each side

Width in reed 12½ in (31 cm)

Finished width 12 in (30 cm)

Weft sett 24 picks per in (2.5 cm)

Warp length 46 in (117 cm)

Number of ends 292 doubled

Designer Helen Frostell

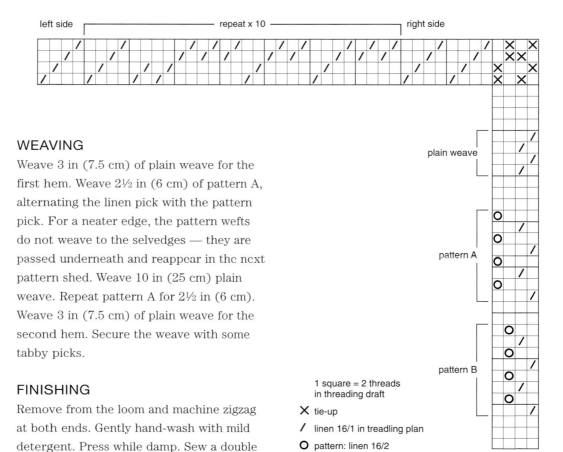

WEAVING

Weave 3 in (7.5 cm) of plain weave for the first hem. Weave 2½ in (6 cm) of pattern A, alternating the linen pick with the pattern pick. For a neater edge, the pattern wefts do not weave to the selvedges — they are passed underneath and reappear in the next pattern shed. Weave 10 in (25 cm) plain weave. Repeat pattern A for 2½ in (6 cm). Weave 3 in (7.5 cm) of plain weave for the second hem. Secure the weave with some tabby picks.

FINISHING

Remove from the loom and machine zigzag at both ends. Gently hand-wash with mild detergent. Press while damp. Sew a double hem with a finished depth of 1 in (2.5 cm).

VARIATION

Pattern B may be incorporated in the design if desired. Weave as for Pattern A.

1 square = 2 threads in threading draft

X tie-up

/ linen 16/1 in treadling plan

O pattern: linen 16/2

Cocoon jacket

This jacket is a simple design that fits most sizes. The fabric is woven in a subtly varying sunset-toned combination of four yarns. Only basic sewing skills are needed, and a sewing machine is not required. It can be finished with a fringe, as pictured, or with a hand-knitted edging (see page 95) or a commercial binding.

Equipment Four-shaft loom, weaving width 28 in (71 cm), ski shuttle, throw shuttle

Technique Plain weave

Warp yarns Bendigo Woollen Mills 2-ply wool yarn (1290 yds/1180 m per 7 oz/200g) in three colours: dusky rose (711), burnt orange (728) and raspberry (714), approximately 746 yds (682 m) of each

Weft yarns Four 1¾ oz (50 g) balls Filatura Di Crosa Multicolour, Colour 4053; and 772 yds (706 m) of 2-ply Bendigo Woollen Mills wool yarn, Colour 714 (raspberry). 16 picks per in (2.5 cm): 8 picks multicolour and 8 picks 2-ply wool

Reed 8 dents per in (2.5 cm)

Weft sett 16 ends per in (2.5 cm). Sley 2 ends per dent

Selvedge Double thread through heddle at each end

Width in reed 28 in (71 cm)

Finished width 26 in (66 cm)

Warp length 5 yds (4.6 m)

Number of ends 448

Designer Wendy Cartwright

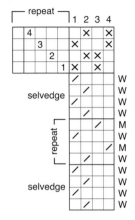

X tie-up
/ treadling plan
W 2-ply wool
M multicolour

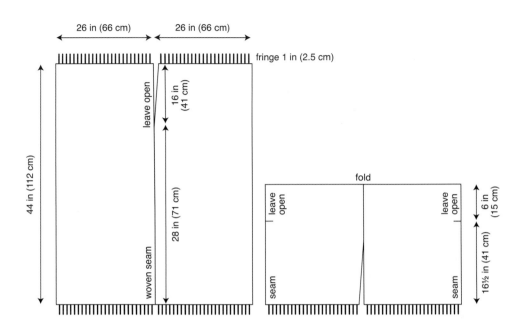

diagram 1 Showing woven seam joining the two lengths of fabric.

diagram 2 Showing folding and seaming.

WINDING THE WARP

Wind a warp 5 yards (4.6 m) long and 28 in (71 cm) wide in all three colours of the 2-ply wool. When winding the warp, the three colours can be wound together with a finger between each to prevent tangling. The three ends can be taken through the cross together and threaded through the reed in the order preferred.

WEAVING

Weave one pick of multicolour and one pick of 2-ply wool as per the treadling plan. Weave two lengths of 50 in (127 cm). Hem stitch (see page 28) at the beginning and end of each piece, and leave 6 in (15 cm)

detail The combination of three colours of 2-ply wool and the multicoloured mohair gives an attractive tonal variation to the plain weave.

between the two pieces for the fringe. Begin and end each piece with four picks of 2-ply wool in plain weave (this makes the hem stitching easier), and then follow the treadling plan. The finished size of each piece will be 26 x 46 in (69 x 117 cm).

FINISHING

Cut the weaving from the loom and wash using a wool-approved detergent. Put the fabric through the spin cycle in a washing machine, steam press and line dry. When dry, steam press again before making up the garment. Sew the pieces together using a woven seam (see page 29) and the mohair yarn as shown in Diagram 1. Fold in half

widthwise as shown in Diagram 2 and sew the side seams, again using a woven seam, leaving 12 in (30 cm) open at the folded end for the armholes. Trim the fringe to about 1 in (2.5 cm).

Rag weave pin cushion

A small, quick project suitable for a beginner weaver. This pattern yields four pin cushions from the one warp, making it ideal for handmade gifts.

Size 5 x 4¾ in (13 x 12 cm)

Equipment Four-shaft loom, ski shuttle, throw shuttle

Technique Plain weave

Warp yarn 22/2 cottolin (3170 yds per lb), colour to suit the cotton strips in the weft

Weft yarns Approximately 240 yds (220 m) 22/2 cottolin (3170 yds per lb), and approximately 1 yd (90 cm) 45 in (114 cm) wide cotton fabric bias cut in ½ in (12 mm) strips

Other materials Firm cotton cloth for backing fabric, cushion filler

Reed 12 ends per in (2.5 cm)

Sett 12 ends per in (2.5 cm)

Selvedge Two ends in each heddle twice on each side

Width in reed 6½ in (17 cm)

Finished width 6 in (15 cm)

Weft sett 5 picks fabric strips plus 10 picks cottolin per in (2.5 cm)

Warp length 50 in (127 cm) for four cushions, including take-up, shrinkage and 26 in (66 cm) loom waste

Number of ends 84

Designer Helen Frostell

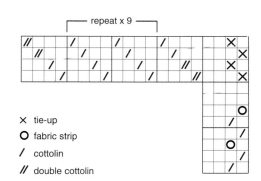

X   tie-up
O   fabric strip
/   cottolin
//   double cottolin

WEAVING

Begin by weaving a ½ in (12 mm) hem allowance in doubled cottolin. Commence the pin cushion with one pick of fabric and two picks of cottolin. Continue for required length. Finish with ½ in (12 mm) in doubled cottolin. Weave a few picks to hold the weave firmly until a machine zigzag can hold it permanently in place.

FINISHING AND ASSEMBLY

Cut the fabric from the loom. Machine zigzag each end. Steam press. Sew the woven top to a base of commercial fabric, right sides together, leaving a gap in one side. Turn the cushion to the right side through the gap and fill with cushion filler. Hand sew the gap to complete the cushion.

WARPING

Wind the two warps separately. For the ground warp, the three ends (one forest green, two navy) can be wound together with a finger between each thread to prevent tangling. The three ends can be taken through the cross together and threaded through the reed in your preferred order. The two ends for the tie down warp are wound the same way and threaded alternately: one black, one purple.

THREADING

The tie down warp is threaded through the reed with the ground warp in every second dent. Once the two warps have been threaded through the reed and heddles, the two warps are beamed together.

WEAVING

Weave two lengths of fabric according to the treadling plan in Diagram 1, each about 60 in (152 cm) long. The fabric is woven at 16 picks per in (2.5 cm): 8 picks ground weft and 8 picks inlay. Leave 5 in (13 cm) of warp at the beginning and 10 in (25 cm) of warp between the two lengths for fringes. Hem stitch each end of each piece while the fabric is on the loom. After finishing, each piece should measure 22 x 56 inches (55 x 142 cm). The loss is due to take-up on the loom and some loss in the finishing process.

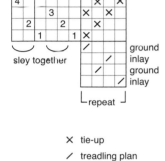

repeat

			1	2	3	4
4					✕		✕
	3			✕		✕
2		2		✕		
	1		1	✕		

sley together

/				ground
	/			inlay
		/		ground
			/	inlay

repeat

✕   tie-up

╱   treadling plan

diagram 1 Design

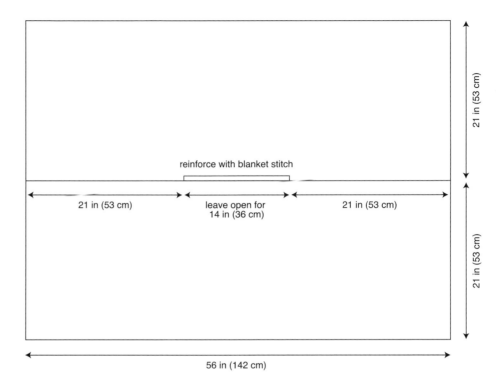

reinforce with blanket stitch

21 in (53 cm)

21 in (53 cm)

21 in (53 cm)

21 in (53 cm)   leave open for   21 in (53 cm)
                        14 in (36 cm)

56 in (142 cm)

diagram 2 Assembling the two pieces

FINISHING

Cut the fabric from the loom and separate
the two pieces. Make a twisted fringe (see
page 29). Hand wash the fabric in a wool-
approved detergent, put through the spin
cycle on your washing machine, steam press
and line dry.

When dry, steam press again.

Hand sew the two together using a woven
seam (see page 29) in the same yarn as
used for the ground weft. Leave 14 in (35
cm) open in the middle for the head hole.
Blanket stitch (see page 29) around each
end of the opening to reinforce.

Triangular off-loom scarf

If you do not have, or do not want to buy, a floor or table loom, items can be woven on a basic frame specially constructed for the purpose. This technique can be used even for fairly large articles such as this scarf.

For your first scarf, it may be wise to use a smooth yarn. This is also an opportunity to use up odds and ends of yarn from other projects; in this case, you may need to alter the sett to achieve a loose, balanced plain weave.

Finished size Approximately 24 in (60 cm) along the straight edge and 33½ in (85 cm) along the diagonal, excluding the fringe

Equipment Specially constructed frame with an outside measurement of 52 x 52 in (130 x 130 cm). Mark the top, bottom and left side at 1 in (2.5 cm) intervals (see diagram on page 59)

Technique Off-loom weave

Warp and weft yarn Hand-dyed bouclé mohair or 12-ply equivalent (the yarn in the pictured example is available from mhawkins8@bigpond.com)

Sett 5 ends per in (2.5 cm)

Weft sett 5 ends per in (2.5 cm)

Designer Mary Hawkins

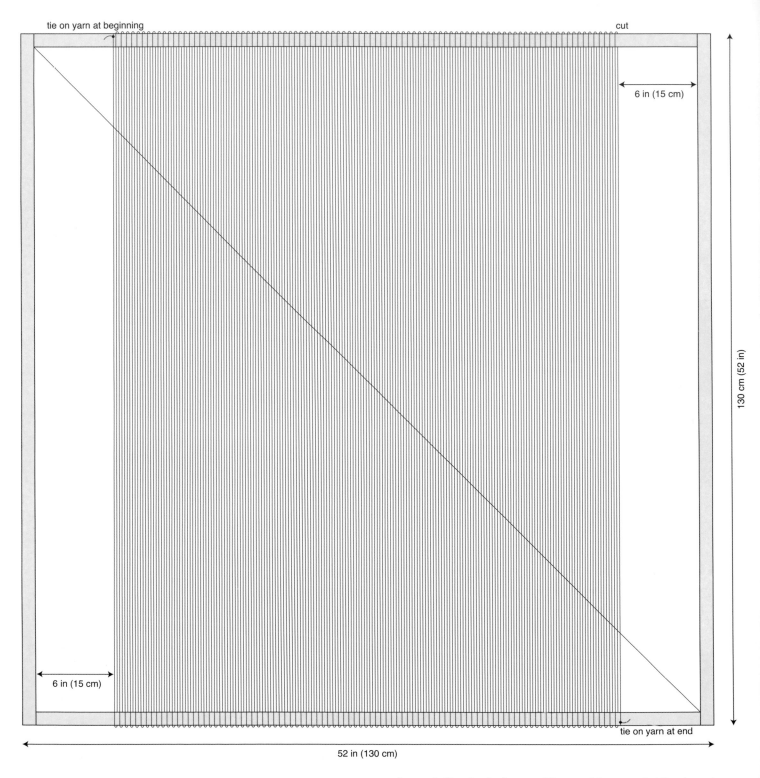

tie on yarn at beginning

cut

6 in (15 cm)

6 in (15 cm)

130 cm (52 in)

tie on yarn at end

52 in (130 cm)

diagram 1 Showing the frame and the complete warp set at 5 ends per in (2.5 cm), plus the diagonal threads over which the weft will be taken.

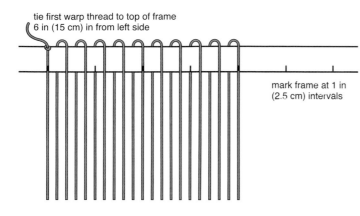

tie first warp thread to top of frame
6 in (15 cm) in from left side

mark frame at 1 in
(2.5 cm) intervals

diagram 2 Detail of the top edge of the frame, showing the start of the threading and the marks along the frame

next warp thread
to be cut off top of frame
and woven across the weft

diagonal threads

commence weaving with
first warp thread on
the right-hand side

these threads remain attached to the bottom of the frame and will later form the fringe

diagram 3 The threads are cut from the top of the frame one at a time and threaded over the diagonal from front to back, then interwoven with the warp threads below the diagonal.

WARPING

Wind a warp set at five ends per in (2.5 cm), going from top to bottom, and starting 6 in (15 cm) in from the left side (see Diagram 2). Tie the start of the thread to the top of the frame, and the end of the thread to the bottom. Once you have finished the threading, run a length of masking tape right across the top of the frame to hold the threads in place once you begin cutting them.

Tape or tie a length of the same yarn diagonally from top left to bottom right. Together with this thread, run a firm, non-elastic, smooth thread (such as fishing line), which will be removed when the scarf is finished. Pull these threads very firmly.

To begin weaving, cut the end thread at the top right of the frame, pulling it out from under the tape. Take this thread and, going over the diagonal threads, weave it across the bottom edge, 6 in (15 cm) from the lower frame. At the same time, this thread remains fixed at the bottom of the frame (see Diagram 3). Use the markings on the left of the frame to ensure that the weft remains perfectly horizontal and at 5 ends per in (2.5 cm). Continue in this manner, so that each end warp thread becomes a weft thread. The extra length of yarn on the left and at the bottom becomes the fringe.

FINISHING

When the weaving is finished, complete the shawl by making a fringe; take bundles of four threads and tie in an overhand knot. Lastly, withdraw the non-elastic smooth thread from the diagonal edge.

Hints

If using a 'hairy' yarn, as in the illustration, it may be necessary to gently beat the weft into position; a table fork works quite well for this purpose.

When weaving with the longer threads, make a "butterfly" by winding the yarn on your hand in a figure-of-eight between the thumb and the little finger.

Ruana

This simple but elegant garment is woven in a shadow weave (see the explanation on page 63). It is constructed from two pieces of fabric that are seamed together at the back only; the fronts are left open so that they can be pinned together, or one side draped across the shoulder.

Size One size fits most; length from shoulder approximately 39 in (100 cm)

Equipment Four-shaft loom, 24 in (60 cm) weaving width, two throw shuttles

Technique Shadow weave

Warp and weft yarns Grignasco Tango: six 1¾ oz (50 g) balls of each of Colours 221 and 218. For the purposes of this project, the green yarn will be referred to as dark and the pink as light

Reed 10 dents per in (2.5 cm)

Sett 10 ends per in (2.5 cm)

Selvedge Double thread through heddle at each end

Width in reed 24 in (60 cm)

Finished width 22 in (55 cm)

Weft sett 10 ends per in (2.5 cm), alternating between the two yarns

Warp length 5½ yds (5.1 m)

Number of ends 240

Designer Wendy Cartwright

detail The combination of pink and green yarns produces a heather-toned effe

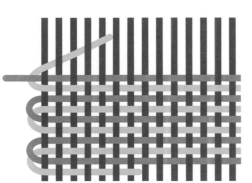

diagram 1 While weaving this shadow weave, you can keep your weft turns even by holding the unused weft taut as you turn the active weft around it.

WINDING THE WARP

Wind a warp with 1 end dark (green) yarn and 1 end light (pink) yarn. When winding the warp, the two colours can be wound together with a finger between each to prevent tangling.

WEAVING

This piece is woven as drawn in. Determining the correct shuttle order for the wefts to interlock at each edge avoids floats up the edges. You can keep your weft turns even by holding the unused weft taut as you turn the active weft around it; see Diagram 1.

Weave two lengths of fabric, each 2 yards 10 in (209 m) long. Leave 5 in (13 cm) of warp at the beginning of the weaving and 10 in (25 cm) of warp between the two lengths, as well as 5 in (13 cm) at the end of the weaving for a fringe. Hem stitch at the beginning and end of each piece while the fabric is still on the loom.

The finished size of each piece should be 22 x 78 in (55 x 198 cm).

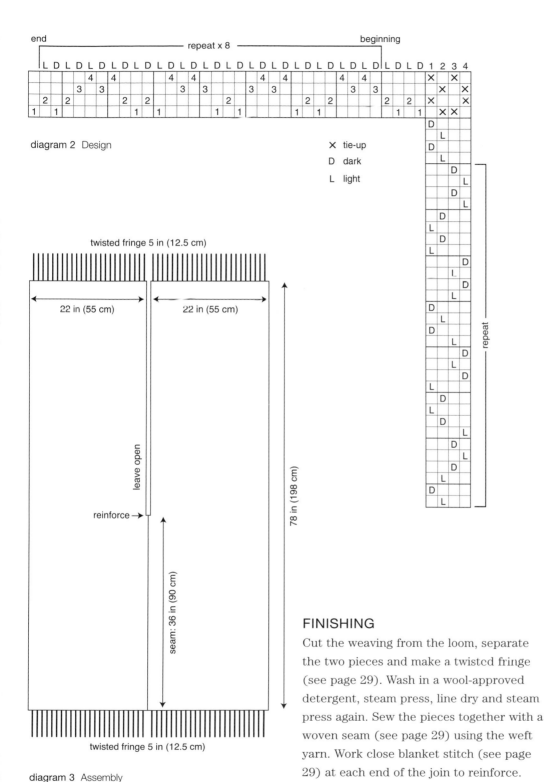

end ← repeat x 8 → beginning

L D L D L D L D L D L D L D L D L D L D L D L D L D L D L D L D 1 2 3 4

diagram 2 Design

X tie-up
D dark
L light

twisted fringe 5 in (12.5 cm)

22 in (55 cm)   22 in (55 cm)

leave open

reinforce →

seam: 36 in (90 cm)

78 in (198 cm)

twisted fringe 5 in (12.5 cm)

repeat

diagram 3 Assembly

Shadow weaves

The shadow weave is a block weave, and is woven warp and weft in a 1 and 1 colouration — that is, one dark and one light end in the warp and the same in the weft. This is a two colour weave. With four shafts you can have four blocks, as follows:

A 1–2
B 3–4
C 2–1
D 4–3

The shaft in bold type carries the dark thread.

FINISHING

Cut the weaving from the loom, separate the two pieces and make a twisted fringe (see page 29). Wash in a wool-approved detergent, steam press, line dry and steam press again. Sew the pieces together with a woven seam (see page 29) using the weft yarn. Work close blanket stitch (see page 29) at each end of the join to reinforce.

Tapestry beret

Another off-loom technique is to use a cardboard template as the basis for the weaving, as in this tapestry beret that incorporates various yarns as well as crocheted bobbles. The brim is knitted in stocking stitch (stockinette).

Finished size Approximately 10¾ in (27 cm) diameter

Equipment 13½ in (34 cm) square thick cardboard; large darning needle; 4 mm circular knitting needle, 60 cm long; 3.5 mm (US 3 or 4/UK 11) or 4 mm (US 5/UK 8) crochet hook; tapestry or weaving needle with a turned-up tip (such as Prym brand, code number 124119)

Technique Off-loom weaving using a cardboard template

Warp yarn 1¾ oz (50 g) ball 4-ply knitting cotton

Weft yarns 8-ply (DK) yarn, 3½ oz (100 g) in Main Colour; and a collection of novelty yarns, such as bouclé, feathery yarn, silk or any designer yarn that will go with your main colour, plus chains of crocheted bobbles (see page 69) in the colours and yarns of your choice

Designer Lynne Peebles

warping Tape the end of the warp yarn to the underside of the template, then begin the threading according to the numbering on the template.

warping, continued Underside of template, showing the completed threading (shown here in a different colour from the previous photograph).

PREPARING THE TEMPLATE

Photocopy Diagram 1 (page 68) at 200 per cent onto A3 (ledger) paper to obtain the correct sized pattern sheet. Photocopy onto two sheets if necessary, and tape together along the point at which the two overlap.

Place the pattern sheet onto the cardboard (make sure the cardboard will not bend easily) and secure with adhesive tape to hold it in place. Using an awl, pierce holes where indicated through the cardboard.

Before removing the pattern sheet, transfer the numbering to the cardboard.

WARPING

Using a long length of 4-ply cotton and a darning needle, start by taping the end to the wrong side of the template, and the bring needle up at the point marked X. Follow the numbering sequence until all holes have been threaded, being careful not to catch the warp threads on the top of cardboard while threading the underside.

When the threading is complete, join the main colour to the warp yarn at the centre. Change to a tapestry needle, then go under the centre warp yarns where they cross each other, and come up ready to commence weaving.

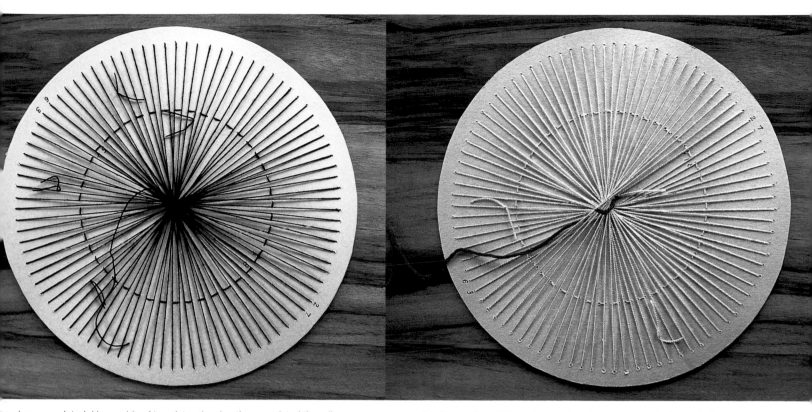

warping, completed Upper side of template, showing the completed threading.

begin weaving Join the main colour of the weft yarn to the end of the warp yarn.

WEAVING

Begin weaving using a twill threading (going under three threads and over one thread), pulling firmly to secure the centre warp threads. Continue in this manner for 1 in (2.5 cm) before changing to one of the fancy yarns. This is the only time the warp yarns will be visible; from now on, the weft yarns should totally cover the warp yarns.

Twill or basket weave will have to be used until the weaving reaches approximately 1½ in (4 cm) from the centre; from then on, plain (tabby) weave — going under one thread and over one thread — can be used.

Pack the weft yarns down as you go, using a comb or your fingers, so that all of the warp yarn is well covered. When you reach the point at which the underside threads start, begin weaving on the underside.

Weave as much of each colour as desired, then change to another yarn, or to a string of crocheted bobbles (see page 69). To end and start a new thread, leave a length of about 2½ in (6 cm) and, using the needle, push the end down to the back of the work. These ends will be stitched in when the weaving is complete and the cardboard has been removed.

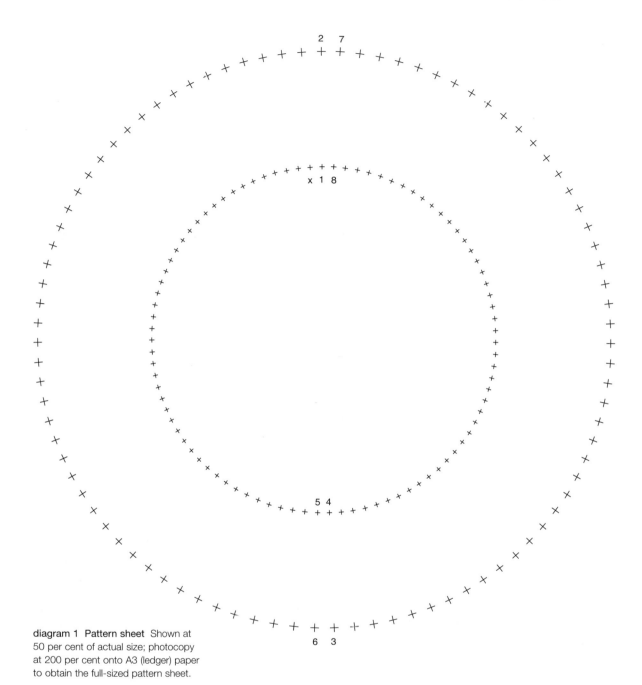

diagram 1 Pattern sheet Shown at
50 per cent of actual size; photocopy
at 200 per cent onto A3 (ledger) paper
to obtain the full-sized pattern sheet.

weaving the centre of the beret The weaving is done in twill for a short distance before plain (tabby) weave is commenced.

weaving the underside of the beret Once the upper side is partly woven, commence weaving on the underside.

MAKING BOBBLES

Using crochet hook, make 6 chain. To make the first bobble, wind yarn over hook (yoh), insert hook into 3rd chain from hook, *(yoh, draw yarn through) twice)*, repeat from * to * four times into same chain. Yoh, draw yarn through all 6 loops on hook, work 1 double crochet (US single crochet), slip stitch into base of stitches (1 bobble made).

To make subsequent bobbles, make 7 chain, then make another bobble in same manner as for first bobble. Make 8 chain, then another bobble. Continue until the bobble chain is the length desired, increasing the distance between the bobbles by one chain each time. Insert a chain of bobbles at any time while progressing with the weaving.

REMOVING CARDBOARD

When the weaving has reached the outer perimeter of both top and underside, remove the cardboard. Do this by bending and tearing it, taking special care not to pull any threads. Scissors are not recommended for the removal of the cardboard, as once any threads are cut, it is almost impossible to repair the weaving.

Using a tapestry needle, weave in all yarn ends on the inside of the beret. Make the knitted brim as instructed at right.

Knitted brim

Using the circular knitting needle, and having the right side of the work facing, pick up 92 stitches around the edge of the beret. Place a marker at the end of the picked-up stitches.

Knit 13 rows in the round, then cast off loosely. Darn the ends of the yarn into the work.

Block the beret if necessary. Using a pressing cloth and light pressure, steam iron the beret.

Wrap with mohair tufts

This wrap is woven in a 2/2 twill with a mohair weft. It is loosely woven, producing a light, nicely draping fabric. The multicoloured tufted yarn used in the weft provides an interesting texture.

Size 76 x 23 in (193 x 65 cm), excluding fringes

Equipment Four-shaft table loom, 24 in (60 cm) weaving width, ski shuttle

Technique 2/2 twill

Warp yarns Bendigo Woollen Mills 2-ply pure wool, approximately 301 yds (275 m) in each of four colours; and one 1¾ oz (50 g) ball Heirloom Jazz

Weft yarn Four ⅔ oz (20 g) balls British Spinners 8-ply (DK) mohair

Reed 8 dents per in (2.5 cm)

Sett 2-ply wool, 16 ends per in (2.5 cm); Heirloom Jazz, 8 ends per in (2.5 cm)

Selvedge 3 ends per dent in the first four and last four dents, using the 2-ply wool

Width in reed 25 in (63 cm)

Finished width 25 in (63 cm)

Weft sett 8 picks per in (2.5 cm)

Warp length 3½ yds (3.2 m)

Number of ends 86 ends in each colour of 2-ply wool, plus 27 of Heirloom Jazz

Designer Wendy Cartwright

WARPING

Wind two warps 3½ yards (3.2 m) long — the first in the four colours of the 2-ply Bendigo wool, winding 86 ends of each colour, and the second with 27 ends of the Heirloom Jazz yarn. The four colours of the 2-ply yarn can be wound together with a finger between each to prevent tangling. When threading, every 13th thread, excluding the selvedges, is Jazz. Thread the selvedge (three ends per dent in the first four dents) then four ends of 2-ply wool, then one end Jazz; continue alternating 12 ends 2-ply and one end Jazz, ending with four ends 2-ply ends and another selvedge of three ends per dent in the last four dents. Thread the 2-ply yarns through the dents in random order.

WEAVING

Leave about 8 in (20 cm) at each end for the fringe. Weave for approximately 78 in (198 cm), hem stitching at the beginning and end of the piece.

FINISHING

Cut the wrap from the loom and make a twisted fringe (see page 29) before washing. Wash in a wool-approved detergent, spin in the spin cycle of your washing machine, steam press and line dry. When dry, steam press again.

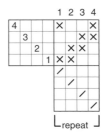

× tie-up
╱ treadling plan

Small fabric bag

Strips of fabric are woven with cotton yarn on four shafts to produce an appealing little bag.

The pictured example uses kimono fabric.

Size 9 x 7¾ in (23 x 19.5 cm)

Equipment Four-shaft loom, ski shuttle, throw shuttle

Technique Plain weave

Warp yarn 16/2 cotton, black

Weft yarn Fabric strips ½ in (12 mm) wide, cut with the grain, alternating with black 16/2 cotton

Other materials Stiffening fabric (for inner bag); lighter fabric (for lining); button or toggle

Reed 12 dents per in (2.5 cm)

Sett 12 ends per in (2.5 cm)

Selvedge 2 ends in each heddle twice on each side. Floating selvedge

Width in reed 10 in (25 cm)

Finished width 9 in (23 cm)

Weft 5 picks fabric, 5 picks cotton per in (2.5 cm) approximately

Warp length 50 in (127 cm), which includes take-up, loom waste and ties

Number of ends 120

Designer Helen Frostell

WEAVING

You will need cotton fabric, such as kimono fabric, for the fabric strips. Cut strips totalling 6 yards (5.5 m). These are folded in half, then ironed, giving ¼ in (6 mm) wide strips. Secure the weave at the beginning with a few picks of cotton. Weave a hem in plain weave (tabby) with doubled 16/2s cotton. Weave for approximately 20 in (50 cm). Weave another plain-weave hem. Secure the weave at the end with a few picks of cotton. Remove the fabric from the loom. Machine zigzag the ends to reinforce.

FINISHING

With wrong sides together, sew the side seams. From the stiffening fabric, make a firm inner bag, slightly smaller than the outer bag, and sew along the top edges; this inner bag gives stability to the bag. Make a lining from a lighter fabric. Attach a strap and a loop for the fastener. Sew the bag and lining together, right sides together, then turn right side out. Steam press. Attach button or toggle.

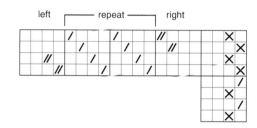

X   fabric strips
/   16/2 cotton
// doubled ends in each heddle

Cushion covers

This complementary pair of cushions uses

a damask weave in subtly contrasting shades

or cotton and linen. The timeless design

would enhance both contemporary and

classic furnishings.

Finished size 17 x 17 in (43 x 43 cm)

Equipment Eight-shaft loom, throw shuttles

Weave Two-block, false damask on eight shafts. Block A on shafts 1 2 3 4, block B on 5 6 7 8

Warp yarns 1110 yds (1015 m) 16/2 cotton at 12,800 m/kg; three different blue to blue-grey colours of similar value. Wind a warp using three threads together, with a finger between each thread to prevent tangling. They are threaded through the reed randomly

Weft yarns 950 yds (869 m) 16/2 linen at 5,190 m/kg; three different dark blue to turquoise colours of similar value, woven randomly using 3 shuttles

Reed 10 dents per in (2.5 cm)

Sett 30 ends per in (2.5 cm)

Threading The colours are selected randomly when threading through the heddles

Selvedges 2 ends per heddle, twice on each side

Width in reed 19 in (48 cm)

Finished width 17 in (43 cm)

Weft sett 26 picks per in (2.5 cm)

Warp length 70 in (178 cm). Seam allowance of ¾–1 in (2–2.5 cm) included

Number of ends 548. This includes the doubled selvedge ends

Designer Helen Frostell

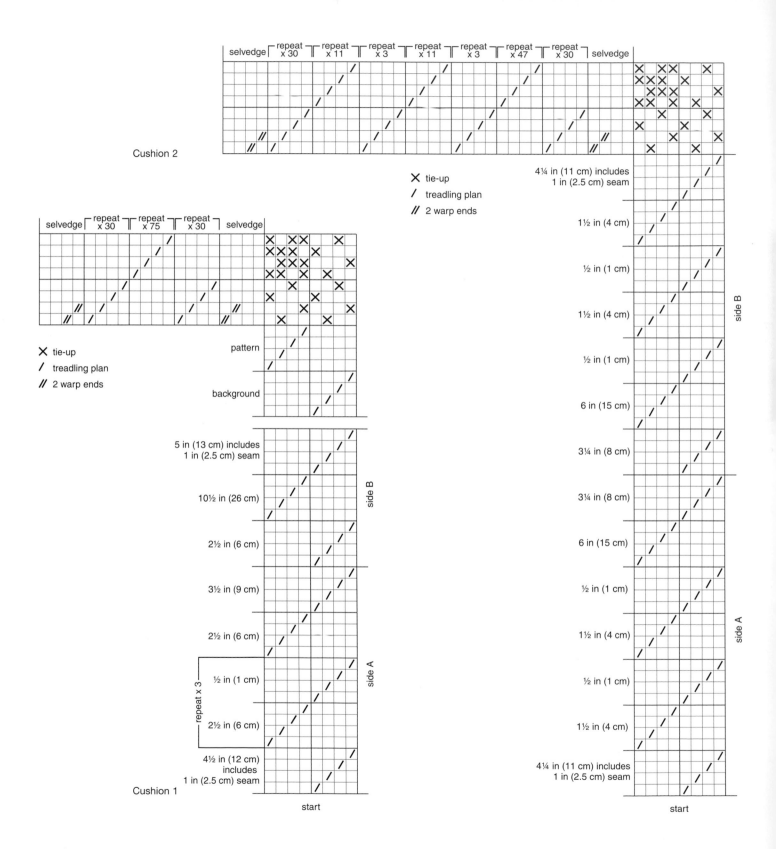

Cushion 2

repeat x 30 | **repeat** x 11 | **repeat** x 3 | **repeat** x 11 | **repeat** x 3 | **repeat** x 47 | **repeat** x 30

selvedge | | | | | | | | selvedge

✕ tie-up

/ treadling plan

// 2 warp ends

Cushion 1

selvedge | **repeat** x 30 | **repeat** x 75 | **repeat** x 30 | selvedge

✕ tie-up

/ treadling plan

// 2 warp ends

pattern

background

5 in (13 cm) includes
1 in (2.5 cm) seam

10½ in (26 cm)

2½ in (6 cm)

3½ in (9 cm)

2½ in (6 cm)

½ in (1 cm)

repeat x 3

2½ in (6 cm)

4½ in (12 cm)
includes
1 in (2.5 cm) seam

side B

side A

start

4¼ in (11 cm) includes
1 in (2.5 cm) seam

1½ in (4 cm)

½ in (1 cm)

1½ in (4 cm)

½ in (1 cm)

6 in (15 cm)

3¼ in (8 cm)

3¼ in (8 cm)

6 in (15 cm)

½ in (1 cm)

1½ in (4 cm)

½ in (1 cm)

1½ in (4 cm)

4¼ in (11 cm) includes
1 in (2.5 cm) seam

side B

side A

start

etail Back of Cushion 1

detail Back of Cushion 2

CUSHION 1

Two different treadling plans are given, 'A' for the front and 'B' for the back. These can be varied as you wish within the limits of the threading plan.

CUSHION 2

Cushion 2 is a variation of cushion 1. You can put on a warp for both cushions. When cushion 1 is completed, it is removed from the loom and a small variation in the threading is done. Ends from shafts 5 6 7 8 are transferred to shafts 1 2 3 4 to give small stripes in the opposite block. This is the threading given for cushion 2. When threading for cushion 1, position extra

heddles on shafts 1 2 3 4 to suit your plan for cushion 2, or make new heddles.

The treadling plan for side 'B' is the reverse of 'A'. This can be varied as you wish within the limits of the threading plan.

WEAVING

Weave a heading to stabilize the weave. Follow the treadling plan for 'A' (front) then continue with 'B' (back) for each cushion. When weaving side 'B', your own pattern may be designed within the limits of the threading. End with a header to prevent fraying. Finish the cushions, following the instructions at right.

Finishing

Remove the fabric from the loom. Machine zigzag the ends of each cushion. Hand wash in warm, soapy water. Rinse well, remove excess water and press while damp.

Fold in half and machine stitch the sides and a short distance on each side of the open end. Place an insert in the cushion and slip-stitch the opening.

Twill wrap

A very elegant garment using a sombre but rich combination of midnight blue and black.

The wool and chenille yarns give a beautifully luxurious texture.

Size 84 x 23 in (214 x 58 cm)

Equipment Eight-shaft loom, ski shuttle

Technique Twill

Warp yarn 1530 yds (1400 m) 2/20 wool (2-ply worsted, 5,600 yds/lb)

Weft yarns 8½ oz (240 g) rayon chenille plied with 700 yds (640 m) fine 3-ply wool (1,300 yds/lb)

Reed 16 dents per in (2.5 cm)

Sett 16 ends per in (2.5 cm)

Selvedge 2 ends twice in each heddle, twice on each side

Width in reed 24 in (60 cm)

Finished width 23 in (58 cm)

Weft sett 8 picks per in (2.5 cm)

Warp length 130 in (330 cm)

Number of ends 384

Designer Helen Frostell

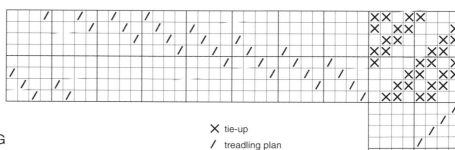

X tie-up

/ treadling plan

WEAVING

Allow 8 in (20 cm) of warp for fringe. Weave eight picks to stabilize the weave. Continue for the required length of 90 in (228 cm). Weave eight picks to stabilize the weave. Remove from loom.

FINISHING

Make a twisted fringe (see page 29) with six threads in each hand. Twist to the right, then let the two cords twist back around each other in the opposite direction. Finish with an overhand knot. Hand wash in warm, soapy water and agitate firmly. Rinse well. Spin dry for 10 seconds. Roll firmly around a tube for 24 hours, then dry flat. Trim the fringes to neaten.

Multi-yarn scarf

This scarf is a good way to use up small amounts of yarn left over from other projects. You can mix textures and different weights of yarn in the same warp. When using yarns of various textures and compositions, it is necessary to keep one constant yarn that is used throughout the piece, at the rate of at least 2–3 threads per in (2.5 cm). This way you avoid a differential take-up, which can occur when different types of yarn are used.

Finished size 7¼ x 58 in (18 x 147 cm)

Equipment Two- or four-shaft loom, ski shuttle

Technique Plain weave on four shafts

Warp yarns Wind a warp 2½ yds (2.3 m) long and 8 in (20 cm) wide. The number of ends depends on yarns used. The base yarn in this scarf is a 2-ply Bendigo Woollen Mills wool in various colours, plus a mixture of yarns (mohair, silk, bouclé, and other fancy yarns). The fine yarns are set at 2 ends per dent and fancy yarns at 1 end per dent in an 8-dent reed

Weft yarns 8-ply mohair at 8 picks per in (2.5 cm). For the weft, choose any yarn used in the warp, or another toning yarn. If using mohair, you need fewer picks per inch

Reed 8 dents per in (2.5 cm)

Selvedge 3 ends per dent for first 3 and last 3 dents, using the 2-ply wool

Width in reed 8 in (20 cm)

Finished width 7½ in 19 cm)

Warp length 2½ yds (2.3 m), or length desired

Number of ends Depends on the yarns used

Designer Wendy Cartwright

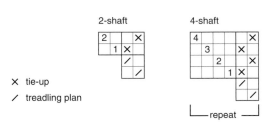

× tie-up
╱ treadling plan

Two designs are shown, for either a two-shaft or four-shaft loom.

WEAVING
Allow about 5 in (13 cm) at each end of the scarf for a fringe. Weave in plain weave for approximately 60 in (152 cm), or the length desired. Hem stitch each end of the scarf (see page 29) while it is on the loom.

FINISHING
Cut the hem-stitched scarf from the loom and make a twisted fringe (see page 29) before washing. Wash in a wool-approved detergent, then spin dry in the spin cycle of the washing machine. Steam press with a cloth, especially if using synthetic yarns, line dry, and steam press again.

Throw from small-loom squares

This throw could be made from a specially

selected array of yarns, but it is also an excellent

way to use up odds and ends of leftover yarn.

The colours don't even have to match or go

together if, as in the pictured example, the

squares are overdyed. In this case, the result is

a beautiful array of reds and greens that make

it very easy to blend and meld the gradation

of colour. This example uses mohair, variegated

yarn, commercial wool and hand-spun yarn; any

piece of yarn that is long enough to complete

a square can be used.

If you do not intend to dye your squares, hand

wash them in a good-quality wool wash, then dry

flat before joining them together.

Finished size Approximately 61 x 73 in
(156 x 185 cm)

Equipment 4-inch (10 cm) small loom (see
pages 30–33); 3 mm (US 2/UK 11) and
3.5 mm (US 3 or 4/UK 9) crochet hooks

Yarn Each square requires 7⅓ yds (6.7 m)
8-ply (DK) or equivalent yarn

Other materials 10½ oz (300 g) 8-ply (DK)
wool for joining the squares and for the
crochet edging; dyes, if overdyeing the
squares (the pictured example uses
Landscape Dyes in red and green)

Number of 4 in (10 cm) squares required 304

Designer Lynne Peebles

Aligning the squares Place each square so that the small loop is at the bottom left and the large loop is at the top right.

Joining Pick up the top right-hand square and the square below it and begin crocheting the two together.

Make the required number of squares. If overdyeing the squares, do this before joining them together. Lay the squares out on a flat surface, in 19 rows of 16 squares, rearranging them until you have a design that pleases you. Note that each square has a small loop at one corner, and diagonally opposite a larger loop. Place all squares in the same position, with the small loop at the bottom left and the large loop at the top right. The wrong side of the squares will now be facing you.

JOINING

Pick up the square at the top right-hand corner of the laid-out squares, and the square below it, right sides together. Join in the 8-ply (DK) yarn at the large loop of the front square. With a 3 mm (US 2/UK 11) crochet hook, work 2 chain, *insert hook into centre of 2 loops of back square and work 1 double crochet (US single crochet), 1 chain, insert hook into the next centre of loops of front square, 1 chain, * repeat from * to * until you reach the end of the two squares, finishing at the small corner loop (the lower left-hand loop) with 3 chain.

Pick up the next two squares and proceed as above until all squares of all rows have been joined horizontally. Next, join the vertical seams in the same manner as for

Joining, continued Showing two pairs of squares joined horizontally.

Joining, continued Showing two pairs of squares joined both horizontally and vertically.

the horizontal seams. At the corners, work 1 chain, slip stitch into the centre chain of the 3 chains, 1 chain, continue to the end.

SHELL CROCHET EDGING

Join in the 8-ply (DK) yarn to the edge of the throw. Use a 3.5 mm (US 3 or 4/UK 9) crochet hook and work in rounds.

Round 1 With right side of throw facing, work 2 double crochets (US single crochets) into the centre of each double loop around the outside edge of the throw. Join with a slip stitch into the first dc of the round.

Round 2 Skip 2 double crochets, make 6 treble crochets (US double crochets) into the next double crochet, *skip 2 dc, 1 dc into next double crochet, miss 2 dc, 6 tr into next dc*, repeat from * to * to end. Join with a slip stitch to the begining of the round.

FINISHING

Sew in all ends of yarn, then press using a pressing cloth.

Flower inlay mats

Hem-stitched linen with a silk inlay creates an elegant set of placemats. Instructions are given for four mats. The same technique could be used with an inlay of your own design.

Size 11¼ x 10½ in (28 x 26 cm)

Equipment Four-shaft loom, throw shuttle

Technique Plain weave with inlay

Warp yarn 16/1 linen. Two threads warped as one. Doubled in heddle and reed = 4 ends per dent

Weft yarn 16/1 linen, 1640 yds (1500 m); inlay: 16 yds (15 m) 2/20s silk

Reed 10 dents per in (2.5 cm)

Sett 20 ends per in (2.5 cm)

Selvedge 3 doubled ends twice in each dent, each side

Width in reed 12 in (30 cm)

Finished width 10¾ in (27 cm)

Weft sett 24 picks per in (2.5 cm)

Warp length 95 in (242 cm) for 4 mats

Number of ends 240

Designer Helen Frostell

WEAVING

Weave a few picks to stablize the weave. Weave for 3 in (7.5 cm) to allow for a 1 in (2.5 cm) doubled hem. Hem stitch, taking four ends per stitch. Insert a spacer of doubled thread, twice (this will later be removed). Weave for 2¾ in (7 cm), then begin the inlay.

INLAY

Pin the pattern under the weave, with the wrong side up. The silk is placed in the last shed used with the linen, following the template. The next shed is linen followed by pattern silk. Continue taking the silk up the side of the pattern. Check the underside with a mirror, as this is the right side. Weave for 2¾ in (7 cm). Insert a spacer as above. Hem stitch as above. Weave for 3 in (7.5 cm) to allow for a 1 in (2.5 cm) doubled hem. Weave a few picks extra to hold the weave firmly.

FINISHING

Remove from the loom. Machine zigzag the edges. Wash in warm to hot water with liquid soap, rinse well and press using a cloth until dry. Remove the spacer. Machine stitch the raw ends and turn under. Bring the fold to the opening left by the spacer to form a 1 in (2.5 cm) doubled hem. Stitch the hem, then press.

× tie-up
∕ linen

Floral inlay pattern Shown at 50 per cent of actual size; photocopy at 200 per cent to obtain the correct size.

Bouclé mohair scarf

The appeal of this very simple plain-weave project lies in the attractive colour shifts of the hand-dyed mohair yarn. Two or more scarves can be warped at a time, if you wish.

Size Approximately 79 x 9 in (200 x 22 cm) excluding fringes

Equipment Four-shaft loom, ski shuttle

Technique Plain weave

Warp and weft yarn 4 oz (120 g) bouclé mohair, approximately 12-ply. The pictured scarf uses a hand-dyed bouclé mohair from mhawkins8@bigpond.com; a commercial equivalent can be substituted

Reed 6 dents per in (2.5 cm)

Sett 6 ends per in (2.5 cm)

Width in reed 10 in (25 cm)

Finished width 9 in (22 cm), approximately

Weft sett 6 ends per in (2.5 cm)

Warp length 2¾ yds (2.5 m)

Number of ends 60

Designer Mary Hawkins

WEAVING

Allow 6 in (15 cm) at each end for the fringe.

Weave in plain weave for approximately 79 in (2 m). Remove fabric from the loom.

Finish with a twisted fringe (see page 29).

Hand wash gently in wool-approved detergent and rinse in fabric conditioner. Spin dry briefly to remove excess moisture. Dry flat.

Fine silk scarf

Here, a geometric design and the lustre of fine silk produce a garment of understated elegance.

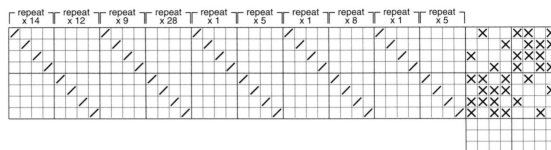

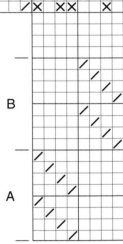

× tie-up
╱ silk

Size 60 x 6¼ in (152 x 16 cm)

Equipment Eight-shaft loom, throw shuttle

Technique Block weave; broken twill using 8 shafts

Warp and weft yarn
2510 yds (2300 m) 60/2 spun silk (15,000 yds/lb).
Block A: 1 2 3 4;
Block B: 5 6 7 8

Warp length 88 in (224 cm)

Reed 12 dents per in (2.5 cm)

Sett 48 ends per in (2.5 cm)

Selvedge 2 ends per heddle twice on each side. Use floating selvedge

Width in reed 7 in (18 cm)

Finished width 6¼ in (16 cm)

Weft sett 48 picks per in (2.5 cm)

Number of ends 336

Designer Helen Frostell

WEAVING

Start lifts 7 4 3 1, or 4 7 5 3 from the left-hand side. Allow 5 in (13 cm) for fringe at each end. Weave each block to correspond with the warp size of each block (as drawn in).

FINISHING

Make a twisted fringe (see page 29) by tightly twisting two groups of eight ends each to the right. Put together and allow to twist with each other to the left. Secure with an overhand knot. Hand wash in warm water with mild detergent. Steam press while damp. Trim fringe.

Variation

This scarf can be woven using 20/2 silk.

Sett 24 ends per in (2.5 cm)
Weft 24 picks per in (2.5 cm)
Number of ends 168 approximately

Adjust the number of ends in the warp blocks by halving the repeats. Where there are no repeats, the 1-2-3-4 remains.

Sleeveless jacket

This jacket is woven in a twill weave in a multi-coloured mohair mix and a fine wool. It is woven in a 3 and 1 twill with a plain-weave pick between each twill pick. This makes for a lighter fabric and uses less of the expensive yarn. The jacket is bound with a hand-knitted bias edging made from the same mohair yarn used in the weaving.

The garment is designed for a loom with a 30-inch (77 cm) weaving width, but it could be woven with a narrower warp of, for example, 17 inches (43 cm) if a wider loom is not available. In this case, there would need to be a seam down the back of the garment.

Size One size fits most; length approximately 32 in (81 cm)

Equipment Four-shaft loom with 30 in (77 cm) weaving width, ski shuttle, throw shuttle

Technique Twill weave

Warp yarns Bendigo Woollen Mills 3-ply pure wool in black and forest green, one 7 oz (200 g) cone of each colour

Weft yarns Four 1¾ oz (50 g) balls Filatura Di Crosa Multicolour, Colour 21, and 1¾ oz (50 g) 2/20s fine wool in purple

Reed 12 dents per in (2.5 cm)

Sett 1 end per dent

Selvedge Double thread each end

Width in reed 30 in (76 cm)

Finished width 28 in (71 cm)

Weft sett 12 picks per in (2.5 cm); 6 picks of multicolour and 6 picks of 2/20s wool

Warp length 3 yds (2.75 m), including approximately 1 yard (90 cm) for take-up and loom waste

Number of ends 360: 120 ends green and 240 ends black

Designer Wendy Cartwright

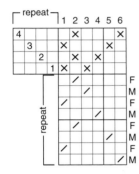

		1 2 3 4 5 6

X tie-up

/ treadling plan

F 2/20s wool

M multicolour

detail Showing both sides of the reversible fabric, and the knitted bias edging.

WARPING

Wind a warp 3 yards (2.75 m) long and 30 in (76 cm) wide, using two ends of black 3-ply wool and one end of green 3-ply wool (a total of 360 yards green and 720 yards black). When winding the warp, the three ends can be wound together with a finger between each to prevent tangling. The three ends can be taken through the cross together and threaded through the reed in the order preferred.

WEAVING

Wind the mohair on the ski shuttle and the ground weft on the throw shuttle. Weave using one pick of mohair followed by one

pick of 2/20s wool as noted in the treadling plan. Weave for 2 yards (1.8 m). Always measure on the loom with the tension off.

FINISHING

Cut the fabric from the loom and overlock or machine zigzag each end. Wash in a wool-approved detergent, rinse well, then put through the spin cycle in the washing machine. Steam press, line dry, then steam press again before cutting the fabric.

CUTTING AND SEWING

Cut the fabric out as per the pattern pieces opposite. Overlock or machine zigzag around all edges before making up the

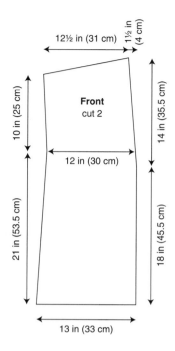

detail A close-up of the weave.

garment. Machine-sew the garment using a ¾ in (2 cm) seam. When the garment has been completed, attach the knitted edging.

KNITTED EDGING

Using the mohair mix yarn and with 4 mm (US 6/UK 8) needles, cast on 9 stitches. Bias knit the strip as follows:

Row 1 Knit 1, knit 2 together, knit to last 2 stitches, increase into next stitch, knit 1.
Row 2 Purl.
Repeat these two rows until the required length is achieved — approximately 6 yards (5.5 m) for the jacket and 22 in (56 cm) for each armhole.

Attach the knitted edging to the garment by machine sewing it to the edges and armholes on the right side. Fold the edging over to the wrong side and hand sew into place.

If you wish, a commercial fabric cut into bias strips can be used instead of the knitted edging.

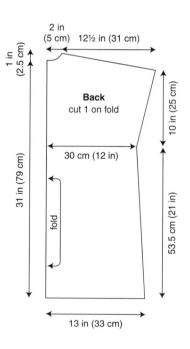

pattern pieces for the jacket For the back, cut one piece on the fold to the dimensions specified; for the front, cut two pieces.

Small table mats

These Japanese-style mats have an attractive ridged effect achieved by using two wefts, one thick and one thin, on a fine warp. Instructions are given for making a set of four mats.

Size 9¼ x 10¼ in (23.5 x 26 cm)

Equipment Four-shaft loom (see Note, below), ski shuttle

Technique Repp weave using four shafts and pedals

Warp yarn Cottolin, two threads used as one

Weft yarns Thick weft: Stranded cotton or ½ in (12 mm) wide rags; Fine weft: 16/2 cotton, similar colour to warp selvedge

Reed 12 dents per in (2.5 cm)

Sett 48 ends per in (2.5 cm)

Width in reed 9¼ in (23.5 cm)

Finished width 9¼ in (23.5 cm)

Weft sett 6 thick and 6 fine picks per in (2.5 cm)

Number of ends 452

Warp length 106 in (2.7 m) for 4 mats, including take-up, loom waste and ties

Designer Helen Frostell

WEAVING

Warp up with two ends of each shade. Weave a 2¼ in (5.5 cm) wide hem in 16/2 cotton on shafts 1 and 3, 2 and 4. Turn under twice to make a double hem.

The mat is woven alternating the thick yarn and the fine yarn. To get a firm edge, roll the thick yarn between your thumb and forefinger, making a firm twist. Enter the thick yarn from the right, then the thin yarn from the left. If the thin weft is under the outside end, enter the shed over the thick weft. If the thin weft is over the outside end, enter the shed under the thick weft.

FINISHING

Secure the weave with machine zigzag. Hand wash gently in warm water. Roll around a tube to remove wrinkles. Allow to dry, then hem.

Note A countermarch loom is ideal for this project, due to the firm beating necessary for the repp weave. Other looms may be used but the result will not be as sturdy.

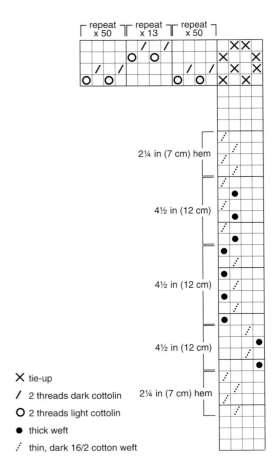

X tie-up
/ 2 threads dark cottolin
O 2 threads light cottolin
● thick weft
⁄ thin, dark 16/2 cotton weft

Ladder yarn and mohair scarf

It is always more economical to wind a warp for two scarves instead of one. In this case, if you wind a 5 yard (4.5 m) warp, you can weave two scarves with one ball of Eros and one ball of Kid Seta.

Size 59 x 7½ in (150 x 19 cm) excluding fringes

Equipment Four-shaft loom, ski shuttle

Technique Plain weave

Warp yarns One 1¾ oz (50 g) ball Eros or other nylon ladder yarn; 240 yds (220 m) of 2/20 wool (60 yds/55 m in each of four colours to match Eros)

Weft yarn 1 oz (25 g) ball Madil Kid Seta mohair/silk mix

Reed 8 dents per in (2.5 cm)

Sett Fine wool: 2 ends per dent; Eros ladder yarn: 1 end per dent

Selvedge 3 ends per dent in first 3 and last 3 dents

Width in reed 8 in (20 cm)

Finished width 7½ in (19 cm)

Weft sett 8 picks per in (2.5 cm)

Warp length 3 yds (2.75 m)

Number of ends 28 ends Eros; 80 ends 2/20 wool (20 ends of each colour)

Designer Wendy Cartwright

WARPING

Wind a warp 3 yards (2.75 m) long and approximately 8 in (20 cm) wide, using one end of Eros nylon ladder yarn and four ends of the 2/20 wool (one end of each colour). The 2/20 wool yarns can be wound together in the warp with a finger between each thread to prevent tangling. The four ends can be wound through the same cross and the colours picked up in order when threading through the reed and heddles.

Thread through the reed as follows: Start with 12 ends of 2/20 wool at 3 ends per dent for the selvedge. Then thread 1 end of Eros and 2 ends of 2/20 wool, and repeat 28 times. Lastly, thread 12 ends of 2/20 wool at 3 ends per dent for the other selvedge. Both warps are wound together on the back roller.

WEAVE

The scarf is woven in plain weave using a very light beat. Leave 5 in (13 cm) of warp at each end of the scarf for a fringe, and hem stitch each end of the scarf while still on the loom (see page 29).

Weave 60 in (153 cm) or length desired.

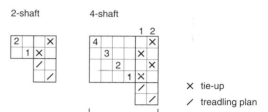

FINISHING

Make a twisted finge (see page 29). Gently hand wash the scarf in a wool-approved detergent, rinse well and put through the spin cycle of the washing machine. Press uisng a cloth, as synthetic yarn can stick to the iron. Press again when dry, using a damp cloth.

Lace weave wrap

Here, an open weave gives a garment with a beautifully soft drape. A variegated mohair yarn

in muted, earthy colours is used on a black background.

Finished size of garment 95 x 21 in
(240 x 53 cm)

Equipment Four-shaft loom with 24 in (60 cm)
weaving width, ski shuttle

Technique Mock leno

Warp yarns 2¾ oz (75 g) 2/22 black
2-ply worsted wool (5,600 yds/lb);
2¾ oz (75 g) contrast yarn in superfine
kid mohair and merino

Weft yarn 2¾ oz (75 g) 2/22 black
2-ply worsted wool (5,600 yds/lb)

Reed 8 dents per in (2.5 cm)

Sett 12 ends per in (2.5 cm)

Selvedge 2 ends three times in each heddle
three times on each side. Omit space in
dent at selvedges, once on each side.
Floating selvedges

Width in reed 24 in (60 cm)

Weft sett 15 picks per in (2.5 cm)

Warp length 130 in (3.3 m)

Number of ends 288

Designer Helen Frostell

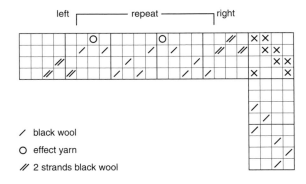

/ black wool

O effect yarn

// 2 strands black wool

THREADING

Sley three ends from each unit in
one dent, then leave the next dent
empty; for example, ends on shafts
1, 2, 1 dented together and ends 3,
4, 3 together, leaving an empty dent
between them.

WEAVING

Allow 8 in (20 cm) of warp at each
end for the fringe. Weave eight
picks to stabilize the weave. These
picks are removed as the fringes are
made. Weave for 95 in (240 cm), or
the required length. Weave eight
picks to stabilize the weave.

FINISHING

Remove the fabric from the loom.
Make a twisted fringe (see page 29)
before washing. Gently hand wash
and spin dry for 10 seconds. Roll
firmly around a tube for 12 hours.
Lightly steam press.

Note The contrast yarn used in the
pictured example is Alpine, a
multicoloured mohair from Touch
Yarns New Zealand, in turquoise
and red. A 12-ply (medium-weight/
aran) mohair may be substituted.

Triangular shawl from small-loom squares

A snuggly garment made from small squares in lush variegated mohair, with a crocheted edging.

Size 90 x 44 in (230 x 110 cm)

Equipment 4 in (10 cm) square small loom (see pages 30–33), 4 in (10 cm) triangular small loom, 3 mm (US 2/UK 11) crochet hook

Yarns Five 1¾ oz (50 g) balls Filatura Di Crosa Multicolour, for squares; 7 oz (200 g) Bendigo Woollen Mills 3-ply Classic Machine Washable Wool, for joining and crocheted edging

Designer Lynne Peebles

detail Showing the crocheted scallop-and-picot edging.

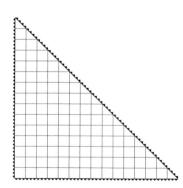

Layout diagram Showing the placement of the motifs.

JOINING MOTIFS

Make 105 squares and 15 triangles. Lay out the motifs on a flat surface, as shown in the diagram at left, rearranging them until you have a design that pleases you. Align and join them as described on pages 85–85, using the crochet hook and the 3-ply (DK) yarn. When all motifs have been joined, join in the 3-ply yarn to the edge of the shawl and begin the crocheted edging.

CROCHETED EDGING

1st Round With right side facing, work in double crochet (US single crochet) around all sides of the shawl, taking care not to stretch the outer edges of the triangles, as these are on the bias. Decrease where necessary to keep the diagonal edge in proportion to the rest of the wrap. On the other two edges, work 1 double crochet into each loop.

2nd Round 1 double crochet into first double crochet, *miss 1 double crochet, into next double crochet work (3 trebles (US double crochets), 1 picot [4 chain, slip stitch into first chain], 3 trebles)*, repeat from * to * on all edges. Join with a slip stitch to the begining of the round.

FINISHING

Sew in all ends of yarn, then press using a pressing cloth.

Reversible cape

This cape is woven in a Theo Moorman weave and is reversible. This weave has two warps and two wefts — a ground warp and a finer tie-down warp for the inlay. The inlay weft is twice as thick as the ground weft. In this fabric, both the ground and inlay wefts are woven from selvedge to selvedge. The ground warp is set for a balanced plain-weave structure and is threaded on shafts 1 and 2. The tie-down warp is an additional warp of much finer threads and is threaded on shafts 3 and 4. The tie-down warp holds the inlay weft in place. It is simple to weave on four shafts and makes a warm, reversible fabric.

This cape is a loose-fitting garment which fits most sizes. It is finished with a bias-knitted edging in mohair yarn, and a narrow collar; the only seams are at the shoulders, which are sewn with a reversible seam.

Size One size fits most; length approximately 30 in (76 cm)

Equipment Four-shaft loom with 24 in (60 cm) weaving width, ski shuttle, throw shuttle, 4.5 mm (US 7/UK 7) knitting needles

Technique Theo Moorman weave using two warps and two wefts

Warp yarns Ground warp: 3-ply pure new wool in light olive green; Tie-down warp: 2-ply pure new wool (6,000m/kg) in olive green (pictured yarns are from Rubi + Lana; see Stockists, on page 111)

Weft yarns Mohair from Touch Yarns New Zealand, Colour 105, approximately 790 yds (723 m), and 2-ply pure new wool (6,000m/kg) in olive green used doubled as ground weft, approximately 1536 yds (1405 m)

Reed 12 dents per in (2.5 cm)

Sett The ground warp is threaded 1 end per dent in a 12-dent reed. The tie-down warp is threaded with the ground warp at 6 ends per dent (one end in every other dent)

Selvedge Double end at each end in the reed and heddle

Width in reed 24 in (60 cm)

Finished width 22 in (55 cm)

Weft sett Approximately 16 picks per in (2.5 cm): 8 picks ground weft and 8 picks mohair weft

Warp length 5 yds (4.6 m)

Number of ends 290 ends ground warp; 144 ends tie-down warp

Designer Wendy Cartwright

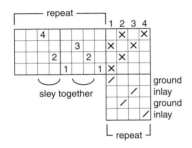

repeat

sley together

ground inlay
ground inlay

× tie-up
/ treadling plan

repeat

detail Showing both sides of the reversible fabric, and the hand-knitted bias edging

Knitted bias edging

The edging is knitted in the mohair yarn. Using 4.5 mm (US 7/UK 7) needles, cast on 9 stitches. Bias knit the strip as follows:

Row 1 Knit 1, knit 2 together, knit to last 2 sts, increase into next st, knit 1.

Row 2 Purl.

Repeat these two rows until the required length (approximately 7 yards/6.4 m) is achieved.

WARPING

Wind two warps, each 5 yards (4.6 m) long and 24 in (60 cm) wide, one in the 2-ply wool for the tie-down warp (720 yards/ 659 m, 144 ends) and one in the 3-ply wool for the ground warp (1440 yards/1317 m, 290 ends). Once the warps are threaded through the reed they can be treated as one warp and threaded and beamed together.

WEAVING

Use a ski shuttle for the mohair and a throw shuttle for the ground weft. Weave approximately 4 yards (3.66 m) of fabric using one pick of mohair and one of 2-ply wool doubled, as per the treadling plan.

Always measure your work on the loom without tension.

FINISHING

Cut the fabric from the the loom and overlock or machine zigzag each end. Hand wash in a wool-approved detergent. Spin dry and then press with a steam iron. Line dry and press again before cutting out the garment as per the pattern pieces opposite. Overlock around all raw edges before making up.

Sew the shoulder seam with a run-and-fell seam so it is reversible. To make a run-and-fell seam, begin by sewing a straight seam.

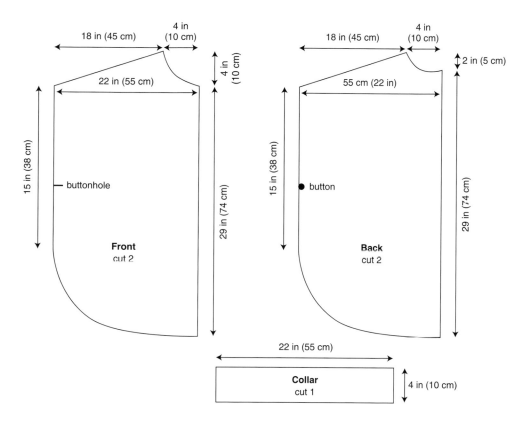

diagram 1 Dimensions of each pattern piece

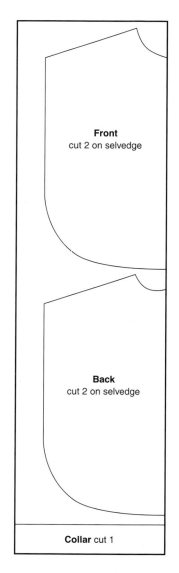

diagram 2 Cutting layout Cut two of each piece on the selvedge.

Open the work out, and press the seam to one side. Trim the inside edge of the seam to reduce bulk, then turn under the outside edge, encasing the inside edge. Stitch the seam down, thus forming a reversible seam.

Sew the two back pieces together using a woven seam (see page 29). Attach the knitted edging to the garment by machine sewing it to all edges of the cape on the mohair side. Fold the edging over to the other side and hand sew into place.

Make two buttonholes on each side edge, 15 in (38 cm) from the shoulder seam as shown in Diagram 1. Sew on two buttons

for each buttonhole so the cape can be reversed. Sew the collar to the neck edge of the cape, leaving 1 in (2.5 cm) extended at each side. Fold the collar over and hand stitch to the other side of the garment. Stitch each end. Make a buttonhole at one end and sew a button on each side of the other end.

Twill silk scarf

A diamond-point twill weave produces a delicately pretty zigzag pattern.

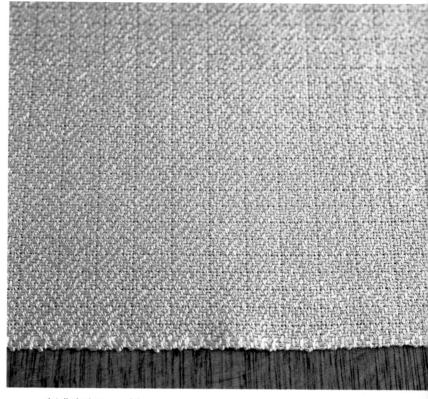

detail A close-up of the weave.

Size 65 x 6¼ in (165 x 16 cm)

Equipment Four-shaft loom, throw shuttle

Technique Twill

Warp and weft yarn 2¾ oz (80 g) 20/2 silk

Reed 12 dents per in (2.5 cm)

Sett 24 ends per in (2.5 cm)

Selvedge 2 ends per heddle twice on each side. Use floating selvedge

Width in reed 7 in (18 cm)

Finished width 6¼ in (16 cm)

Weft sett 24 picks per in (2.5 cm)

Warp length 95 in (240 cm)

Number of ends 172

Designer Helen Frostell

WEAVING

Allow 5 in (13 cm) at each end for the fringe. Weave six picks to stabilize the weave. These are removed as the fringes are made. Continue for the required length of 70 in (178 cm). Weave six picks to stabilize the weave. Remove from loom.

FINISHING

Make a twisted fringe (see page 29) using two groups of eight ends each. Wash in warm water with mild detergent. Steam press while damp. Trim fringes.

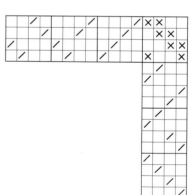

Index

Stockists

Bendigo Woollen Mills
Lansell St, Bendigo VIC 3550
Australia. Ph (03) 5442 4600

Hand-dyed mohair yarn
available from Mary Hawkins,
mhawkins8@bigpond.com

Rubi + Lana
Shop 21, 767 Pacific Hwy,
Gordon NSW 2072 Australia
Ph (02) 9499 9711

Small weaving looms hand-
crafted in Australian silky oak
available from Ron and Linda
Stewart (+61 2) 9543 1228

Touch Yarns New Zealand
www.touchyarns.com

Published in 2007 by Murdoch Books Pty Limited
www.murdochbooks.com.au

Murdoch Books Australia
Pier 8/9, 23 Hickson Road, Millers Point NSW 2000   Phone: +61 (0) 2 8220 2000   Fax: +61 (0) 2 8220 2558

Murdoch Books UK Limited
Erico House, 6th Floor, 93—99 Upper Richmond Road, Putney, London SW15 2TG
Phone: +44 (0) 20 8785 5995   Fax: +44 (0) 20 8785 5985

Chief Executive: Juliet Rogers
Publisher: Kay Scarlett

Concept: Tracy Loughlin
Art direction: Vivien Valk
Designer: Jacqueline Richards
Project manager and editor: Janine Flew
Project designers and makers: Wendy Cartwright, Helen Frostell, Mary Hawkins, Lynne Peebles
Techniques text (pages 6—29): Wendy Cartwright
Photographer: Natasha Milne
Stylist: Sarah O Brien
Production: Adele Troeger

National Library of Australia Cataloguing-in-Publication Data
Weave : designs. Includes index.
ISBN 978 1 74045 978 5.
1. Weaving - Patterns. I. Cartwright, Wendy. (Series : Handmade style). 746.14041

The Publisher would like to thank the following for their assistance in the preparation of this book: The Society of Arts
and Crafts of New South Wales and its members; Amanda McKittrick; Ron Stewart, for supplying the small looms
pictured on page 11 and granting permission to reproduce the instructions on how to use them, on pages 30—33.

Printed by C&C Offset Printing Co., Ltd. PRINTED IN CHINA.
Reprinted 2007.